NEW ESSAYS ON
MY ÁNTONIA

D0148955

The American Novel series provides students of American literature with introductory critical guides to great works of American literature. Each volume begins with a substantial introduction by a distinguished authority on the text, giving details of the work's composition, publication history, and contemporary reception, as well as a survey of the major critical trends and readings from first publication to the present. This overview is followed by a group of new essays, each specifically commissioned from a leading scholar in the field, which together constitute a forum of interpretative methods and prominent contemporary ideas on the text. There are also helpful guides to further reading. Specifically designed for undergraduates, the series will be a powerful resource for anyone engaged in the critical analysis of major American novels and other important texts.

My Ántonia is the Cather novel that is most often taught in high school and college courses, and the one that most readers try first when they approach Cather. It is at once her most autobiographical novel and her most aesthetically complex; it can be enjoyed both for its simple, pure prose and for its literary depth. The essays in this volume place the novel in the context of American literary history, African American music, feminist theory, and Southern writing, offering illuminating ways of reading Cather's best-known work.

Sharon O'Brien is John Hope Caldwell Professor of American Cultures at Dickinson College.

★ The American Novel ★

GENERAL EDITOR

Emory Elliott
University of California, Riverside

Other works in the series:

The Scarlet Letter
The Great Gatsby
Adventures of Huckleberry Finn
Moby-Dick
Uncle Tom's Cabin
The Last of the Mohicans
The Red Badge of Courage
The Sun Also Rises
A Farewell to Arms
The American
The Portrait of a Lady
Light in August
The Awakening
Invisible Man
Native Son
Their Eyes Were Watching God
The Grapes of Wrath
Winesburg, Ohio
Sister Carrie
The Rise of Silas Lapham
The Catcher in the Rye
White Noise
The Crying of Lot 49
Walden
Poe's Major Tales
Rabbit, Run
Daisy Miller and The Turn of the Screw
Hawthorne's Major Tales
The Sound and the Fury
The Country of the Pointed Firs
Song of Solomon
Wise Blood
Go Tell it on the Mountain
The Education of Henry Adams
Go Down, Moses
Call It Sleep

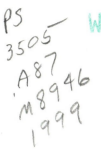
New Essays on
My Ántonia

Edited by
Sharon O'Brien

CAMBRIDGE
UNIVERSITY PRESS

PUBLISHED BY THE PRESS SYNDICATE OF THE UNIVERSITY OF CAMBRIDGE
The Pitt Building, Trumpington Street, Cambridge CB2 IRP, United Kingdom

CAMBRIDGE UNIVERSITY PRESS
The Edinburgh Building, Cambridge CB2 2RU, UK http://www.cup.cam.ac.uk
40 West 20th Street, New York, NY 10011-4211, USA http://www.cup.org
10 Stamford Road, Oakleigh, Melbourne 3166, Australia

First published 1999

Printed in the United States of America

Typeset in Meridien 10/13 pt. in Penta [BV]

*A catalog record for this book is available from
the British Library*

Library of Congress Cataloging-in-Publication Data
New essays on My Ántonia / edited by Sharon O'Brien.
p.   cm. – (The American novel)
Includes bibliographical references.
ISBN 0-521-45275-9 (hb)   ISBN 0-521-45905-2 (pbk)
1. Cather, Willa, 1873–1947. My Ántonia.   2. Frontier and pioneer
life in literature.   3. Women pioneers in literature.   4. Nebraska –
In literature.   I. O'Brien, Sharon.   II. Series.
PS3505.A87M89454   1998
813'.52 – dc21   97-39168

ISBN 0 521 45275 9 hardback
ISBN 0 521 45905 2 paperback

Contents

Contents

5
"It Ain't My Prairie":
Gender, Power, and Narrative in
My Ántonia
MARILEE LINDEMANN
page 111

Series Editor's Preface

In literary criticism, the last twenty-five years have been particularly fruitful. Since the rise of the New Criticism in the 1950s, which focused attention of critics and readers upon the text itself – apart from history, biography, and society – there has emerged a wide variety of critical methods which have brought to literary works a rich diversity of perspectives: social, historical, political, psychological, economic, ideological, and philosophical. While attention to the text itself, as taught by the New Critics, remains at the core of contemporary interpretation, the widely shared assumption that works of art generate many different kinds of interpretations has opened up possibilities for new readings and new meanings.

Before this critical revolution, many works of American literature had come to be taken for granted by earlier generations of readers as having an established set of recognized interpretations. There was a sense among many students that the canon was established and that the larger thematic and interpretative issues had been decided. The task of the new reader was to examine the ways in which elements such as structure, style, and imagery contributed to each novel's acknowledged purpose. But recent criticism has brought these old assumptions into question and has thereby generated a wide variety of original, and often quite surprising, interpretations of the classics, as well as of rediscovered works such as Kate Chopin's *The Awakening,* which has only recently entered the canon of works that scholars and critics study and that teachers assign their students.

The aim of The American Novel Series is to provide students of American literature and culture with introductory critical guides to American novels and other important texts now widely read and studied. Usually devoted to a single work, each volume begins with an introduction by the volume editor, a distinguished authority on the text. The introduction presents details of the work's composition, publication history, and contemporary reception, as well as a survey of the major critical trends and readings from first publication to the present. This overview is followed by four or five original essays, specifically commissioned from senior scholars of established reputation and from outstanding younger critics. Each essay presents a distinct point of view, and together they constitute a forum of interpretative methods and of the best contemporary ideas on each text.

It is our hope that these volumes will convey the vitality of current critical work in American literature, generate new insights and excitement for students of American literature, and inspire new respect for and new perspectives upon these major literary texts.

Emory Elliott
University of California, Riverside

1

Introduction

SHARON O'BRIEN

"LIFE BEGAN FOR ME," Willa Cather once said, "when I ceased to admire and began to remember."[1] Her artistic power was also born when she moved from admiration to memory. But this was a long process. Cather began writing fiction as an undergraduate at the University of Nebraska in the early 1890s; in her first novel, *Alexander's Bridge* (1912), she was still writing as an admirer of the great writers who preceded her. Honoring in particular the fiction of Henry James, whom she once referred to as the "mighty master of language," Cather set her novel in the Jamesian drawing rooms of London and Boston.[2]

In *O Pioneers!*, published a year later in 1913, Cather began her literary breakthrough, returning to the Nebraska cornfields and inventing a character new to American fiction – a strong, creative woman who (unlike the heroines of Henry James) is not rebuked for her independant-mindedness. Cather continued to take what she called "the road home" in *The Song of the Lark* (1915), her novel of a woman artist's emergence from a Western background much like her own.[3]

It was in *My Ántonia* (1918), however, that Cather most fully transformed memory into art. She dedicated the novel to two friends of childhood, Carrie and Irene Miner, "in memory of affections old and true." Many friends from her Red Cloud childhood inspired characters in her novel – most notably the Bohemian "hired girl," Annie Pavelka, who was the source for Ántonia Shimerda.[4] The story of narrator Jim Burden's childhood uprooting from Virginia and transplanting to Nebraska was also Cather's own. Of course the novel is fiction, drawing on life but

1

transforming it into art. Yet in *My Ántonia* Cather not only drew more deeply on her Nebraska past than she ever would again; she also made the role of memory in shaping the past central to the novel's design – memory infiltrated by the transformative energies of imagination and desire.

Cather spent most of her childhood and adolescence in Red Cloud, a small Nebraska prairie town, and graduated from the University of Nebraska in Lincoln in 1895. She then moved east, working as a journalist and a teacher in Pittsburgh and moving to New York City in 1906 to take up a staff position at *McClure's Magazine.* Eventually Cather became managing editor, before plunging full time into writing in 1912. Investing herself in a literary and professional world dominated by East Coast values, Cather at first saw no way to link her regional past with her hopes for an artistic future. During the early 1900s, she said later, Nebraska was considered "declassé" as a literary background by snobbish Eastern critics; no one who was anyone "cared a damn" about Nebraska, no matter who wrote about it.[5]

Willa Cather was shaped by nineteenth-century assumptions about gender as well as region. Confronted by an ideology of femininity that associated womanhood with domesticity – not authorship – for many years Cather associated artistic greatness with masculinity. She did not have "much faith in women in literature," she claimed in 1895. "As a rule, if I see the announcement of a new book by a woman, I – well, I take one by a man instead. . . . I have noticed that the great masters of letters are men, and I prefer to take no chances when I read."[6] But as long as Cather did not have much faith in women writers, she could not have much faith in her own literary talent. Her acceptance of a patriarchal culture's disparagement of women writers inevitably delayed her own artistic emergence.

Central to Cather's evolution as woman and writer was the respected Maine writer Sarah Orne Jewett, whom Cather met in 1908. Jewett was Cather's guide at the crucial transitional moment in her life, supporting her as she found both her voice as a writer and her literary road home to Nebraska. A woman and a gifted writer herself, Jewett helped Willa Cather to see that these identities could coexist in herself.

2

Although Jewett – best known for *The Country of the Pointed Firs* (1896) – outranked the younger writer in literary achievements, their brief friendship, which lasted until Jewett's death in 1909, was marked by mutuality. Jewett was mentor to Cather's emerging creativity; at the same time, Cather gave Jewett the chance to find a literary heir. "One of the few really helpful words I ever heard from an older writer," Cather said in 1922, "came from Jewett, who said, Of course, one day you will write about your own country. In the meantime, get all you can. One must know the world *so well* before one can know the parish."[7]

Cather dedicated *O Pioneers!* to Jewett, and she easily could have dedicated *My Ántonia* as well, for the novel reflects both Jewett's advice and her example. In *My Ántonia* Cather returns to her own country for inspiration, and there she, like Jewett, finds creative power in the folk art of storytelling, a creative inspiration that we can trace in Willa Cather's life back to her birthplace in Virginia.

* * * * *

Although we associate Willa Cather with the Nebraska landscape she evokes so powerfully in *My Ántonia*, she spent her childhood in the enclosed green world of Virginia's Shenandoah Valley. Born in the small farming community of Back Creek, Virginia, in 1873, the eldest of seven children of Charles and Virginia Cather, Willa Cather found her first introduction to narrative in the storytelling of local women who came to the Cather farmhouse, Willow Shade, to help with the canning, preserving, and quilting. Many of these stories Willa Cather "remembered all her life," her partner Edith Lewis recalls; they would finally shape the last book published in her lifetime, *Sapphira and the Slave Girl* (1940), the novel in which she most fully returned to her Southern inheritance.[8]

In 1883 Charles Cather decided to join his father and brother, who were farming in Nebraska. So the young Willa was uprooted from the gentle, sheltering landscape she loved and "thrown out" into a country "as bare as a piece of sheet iron." She experienced an "erasure of personality" during her first months in Nebraska, almost dying, she later said, from homesickness.[9] In *My Ántonia* Cather gives this experience of uprooting and transplantation to Jim Burden, who shares her initial sense of Nebraska's bleak immensity:

There seemed to be nothing to see; no fences, no creeks or trees, no hills or fields. If there was a road, I could not make it out in the faint starlight. There was nothing but land: not a country at all, but the material out of which countries are made. No, there was nothing but land. . . . (7)

Eventually Cather came to love her new home. The wide expanse of prairie gave her a sense of freedom rather than annihilation, and her exhilaration with the West's open spaces lasted a lifetime. "When I strike the great open plains, I'm home," she would say. "That love of great spaces, of rolling open country like the sea – it's the grand passion of my life."[10]

Helping Cather to feel at home on the prairies were the immigrant farmers who had come to the Midwest to start over; like the young Cather, they were surviving the trauma of uprooting and resettlement. She was surrounded by a far more varied ethnic mix of people than she had experienced in the more homogenous culture of the Shenandoah Valley – Scandinavians, French, Russians, Germans, and Bohemians farmed alongside native-born Americans. Cather particularly loved to spend time with the immigrant pioneer women, who replaced the storytellers of Willow Shade, telling her stories about their European homelands, just as Ántonia tells Jim about Bohemia.

Even after the Cather family moved to the small prairie town of Red Cloud in 1884, Cather kept up these attachments. She also found herself drawn to the daughters of these immigrant women, the "hired girls" like Annie Sadilek, later Annie Pavelka. In Red Cloud Cather formed other new friendships with native-born Americans, in particular the daughters of the Miner family, Carrie and Irene. In *My Ántonia* Carrie is transformed into Frances Harling, and Mrs. Miner, for whom Annie Sadilek worked, becomes Mrs. Harling – the only exact fictional portrait Cather claimed to have drawn. Cather also drew on her grandparents William and Caroline Cather for the portrait of Jim Burden's grandparents; and an occasional visitor to Red Cloud, the

4

black pianist Blind Boone, became the model for the novel's Blind d'Arnault.

Transforming her own experiences into Jim Burden's narrative, reworking Nebraska friends and acquaintances into the fictional weave, in this novel Cather drew most profoundly on her childhood memories – which may be the reason why, of all her fiction, *My Ántonia* was the novel about which she cared most deeply.

Yet *My Ántonia* is neither a childhood memoir nor a "young adult" book (despite its popularity on high school reading lists): it is a midlife novel about childhood. Like Jim Burden, Cather needed emotional, aesthetic, and chronological distance from her Nebraska past in order to write about it. Cather's creative process was based on loss. In order to write, she needed to feel the desire to possess and recreate what was missing or absent. So the creative process for her was joyous in that she could, in memory and imagination, bring to life what was gone; but it was also always and inevitably imbued with sadness. What is lost can be remembered and transformed into art, but it cannot ever be recaptured. We can see this doubleness in Jim's first-person narrative, which dramatizes Cather's own creative process. During the act of writing the past comes alive for him again: phrases like "I can see them now," or "they are with me still" recur throughout the novel. "They were so much alive in me," Jim says of the Black Hawk friends he brings with him in memory to Lincoln "that I scarcely stopped to wonder whether they were alive anywhere else, or how" (262). And yet there is a melancholy tone to *My Ántonia,* reflected in the epigraph from Virgil – "*optima dies prima fugit,*" the best days are the first to flee. Some losses are permanent; time, change and death must be accepted if we are also to accept life.

Willa Cather was well aware of the reality of loss during the writing of *My Ántonia.* In 1916 Isabelle McClung, her closest friend, creative companion, and romantic love of her life, announced that she was going to marry the violinist Jan Hambourg. This was a terrible blow to Cather. She had lived with Isabelle during her Pittsburgh years, and after her move to New York had returned to Pittsburgh for long visits. Isabelle had known how to nurture her friend's creativity; Cather wrote most of *O Pioneers!* and *The Song of the Lark* in the sanctuary Isabelle lovingly created for her. In her art, Cather never wrote directly of the love between women – she was well aware of her culture's definition of lesbianism as "unnatural" – but in life her deepest emotional bonds would always be with women. Of these, her bond with Isabelle was the most significant. To lose Isabelle was like a divorce, or a death. When she spoke with her friend Elizabeth Sergeant about the marriage, her eyes were "vacant" and her face "bleak." "All her natural exuberance had drained away," Sergeant remembers.[11]

Throughout the spring of 1916 Cather remained grieving and depressed. She had an idea for a new novel (which would later become *My Ántonia*) but no interest or energy: her creativity was as dead as Nebraska's winter landscape seems to Jim Burden.

But Cather was resilient in both her life and her art. In the summer of 1916 she travelled west and spent several months in Red Cloud, renewing attachments with family and old friends, including Annie Pavelka – the inspiration for Ántonia and the spark for her next novel. Isabelle's marriage was a hard blow, and she would always feel the loss, but the rest of the world was still there, as was Cather's creative power.

When Cather returned to New York, *My Ántonia* was ready to emerge. She spent several months writing happily in the city before finding a new summer retreat to replace Pittsburgh – the Shattuck Inn in Jaffrey, New Hampshire. There she pitched a tent in a friend's meadow. This became the morning retreat where she wrote *My Ántonia* – "an ideal arrangment," recalls Edith Lewis:

The tent was about half a mile from the Inn, by an unused wood road, and across a pasture or two. Willa Cather loved this solitary half-mile walk through the woods, and found it the best possible prelude to a morning of work. She wrote for two or three hours every day, surrounded by complete silence and peace.[12]

We can see Cather's recent as well as remote experiences of loss and change threading their way through *My Ántonia* – not just in Jim's yearning for a golden past and Ántonia's transformation from a "lovely girl" into a "battered woman" (353), but also in violent and disturbing episodes that may reflect Cather's anger at loss: the suicide of Mr. Shimerda, Ántonia's seduction and betrayal, the brutal story of Pavel and Peter, the villainy of Wick Cutter.

But Cather's own renewal of creative energy is also evident in the novel it produced. In *My Ántonia* she affirms the power of people to weave the sadness of loss – of homelands, of loved friends and family, of childhood, of the past – into the web of ongoing life by telling stories. Foremost is Cather's own story, the novel we read; but there is also Jim's story, the manuscript we read after the Introduction; and within Jim's story are many other stories, like the Bohemian folk tales Ántonia tells, the story of Pavel and Peter (which she translates for him), the story of Wick Cutter's death (which her children tell to Jim), the story of Ántonia's seduction as told by the Widow Steavens, the stories Ántonia and her children tell while they look at old photographs, and the stories of Jim that Ántonia has been telling her children during his twenty-year absence.

Just as the novel demonstrates the connection between loss and creativity, so it shows us the link between the oral and the written, the folk narrative and the novel. In *My Ántonia* Cather honors the oral tradition of storytelling that nourished both the child and the writer. But oral narrative is more vulnerable to time and change than written narrative; after a while, stories may die out if there are no inheritors to keep telling them. And written narratives can also disappear if they do not find an audience through the act of publication.

Willa Cather was able successfully to transform the oral narrative into written form, thus giving one kind of permanence to the stories she heard, inherited, and created. By 1917, she was a well-known writer with literary power and authority. So she was also able to negotiate the transformation of her written manuscript into a published novel that embodied her own creative vision, guiding *My Ántonia* from the inner realm of the writer's desk into the outer world of contracts, book design, and advertising. The novel's publishing history is a fascinating one, and reveals how Cather struggled to unite the role of writer with that of author, and to integrate the private space of composition with the public space of commerce.

* * * * *

Cather's first publisher was the Boston-based firm of Houghton Mifflin, inheritors of Ticknor and Fields, the nineteenth-century Boston publishers who brought Hawthorne, Emerson, Longfellow, Lowell, Jewett, and Stowe to the American reading public. Houghton Mifflin thus was associated in Cather's mind both with her mentor Sarah Orne Jewett (and with Jewett's companion Annie Fields, widow of James Fields, partner in the original publishing company) and with the New England–dominated American literary canon. So in 1912, when Cather brought *Alexander's Bridge* to Houghton Mifflin, she was associating herself with publishers who were the inheritors and disseminators of American literary culture. In joining their literary family, Cather was becoming a descendant of Hawthorne and Emerson as well as of Jewett.

The publishing industry in the early twentieth century, like the author's relationship to editor and publisher, was a complex, contradictory enterprise, at once public and private, commercial and aesthetic. Houghton Mifflin, for example, viewed itself not as a corporation but as a cultural institution dedicated to furthering American letters, fostering authors, and bringing good books to the general reader. (Of course, it was not dedicated to these aims at the expense of profit.) Publishing companies like Houghton Mifflin liked to imagine themselves more as families than as corporate enterprises, seeking to honor noneconomic motives and relationships while at the same time managing healthy sales. The uneasy compromise such publishers envisioned between their commerical and familial motives is suggested by the very term they used to describe themselves: "houses" rather than "companies" (this older image is still anachronistially preserved in "Random House" and its family-dwelling logo). Publishing houses like Houghton Mifflin hoped for familial relationships between editors and authors, based on mutual respect for writing rather than the profit motive. Indeed, when Cather's editor Ferris Greenslet wrote her of his sadness at her decision to leave Houghton Mifflin for Knopf, he used the imagery of home and family: perhaps someday she would return, he hoped – the latch-string at Park Street would always be open, and she could come back any time she wished.[13]

During her Houghton Mifflin years Cather at first played the deferential role of the grateful daughter to Ferris Greenslet, welcoming his editorial suggestions and praising his advice. But as she began to accrue positive reviews for *O Pioneers!* and *The Song of the Lark*, she became more assertive and began to challenge the publisher's inadequacies. Cather shared Houghton Mifflin's sometimes contradictory definition of the meaning of the book. She wanted her books to sell, so that she could support herself as a full-time writer. Yet she did not want her books to be treated as interchangeable commodities, or to be grouped with popular writers who turned out one formulaic best seller after another. She wanted to be an individual artist, and for each of her novels to have its own unique vision; at the same time she wanted Houghton Mifflin to promote her work actively and to make her a writer honored by the press and supported by the public.

When she began writing *My Ántonia* in 1916, Cather was beginning to be unhappy with Houghton Mifflin, suspecting that her publisher was committed neither to the aesthetic quality nor to the commercial success of her books. Disturbed by what she considered Houghton Mifflin's careless attitude toward her books' appearance, she wanted to influence both design and production – cover, book jacket, typeface, paper, binding.

Cather's desire to determine the aesthetic shape of the book as a whole reached a height with *My Ántonia*. In addition to stating her preferences for the cover (darker blue than *The Song of the Lark*) and book jacket (bright yellow, with heavy black lettering), Cather commissioned a series of line drawings from the artist W. T. Benda to illustrate her manuscript. Born in Bohemia, Benda had spent a good deal of time in the American West, and Cather felt his imaginative vision was consonant with hers. When Houghton Mifflin balked at paying for Benda's drawings, Cather became increasingly frustrated at what she considered her publisher's stingy disregard for her aesthetic decisions. Cather had originally imagined twelve illustrations, but Houghton Mifflin agreed to such a small payment – $150 – that she could commission only eight.

Her correspondance with editor Ferris Greenslet and Houghton Mifflin's art department reveals how strongly Cather wanted to shape *My Ántonia* visually as well as verbally. Benda executed the sketches according to Cather's guidelines: she wanted simple pen-and-ink drawings that would resemble old woodcuts, because she knew the purity of her novel would be jarred by illustrations that seemed too flashy, slick, or sentimental. At first she thought she wanted "head and tail" pieces – illustrations inserted at the beginning or end of a chapter – but then decided that each illustration required a separate page, adding to the impression of woodcuts. The blank space was also part of the design, Cather decided; she told the art department to print the illustrations low on the page, so the reader could sense the presence of air and space overhead. She also wanted the drawings on right-hand pages, juxtaposed to the part of the text they illustrated, and printed in the same black ink.[14]

Even though Houghton Mifflin eventually followed her instructions, Cather felt her publisher never understood how aesthetically central the Benda illustrations were to her novel's design. After leaving Houghton Mifflin Cather had to fight to keep the Benda illustrations in later editions. The publisher dropped the illustrations in a cheap 1930 reprint, which Cather considered an unauthorized edition of *My Ántonia*. In 1937 Ferris Greenslet wanted to replace Benda's sketches with fancier color plates by Grant Wood, finally backing down after Cather objected strenuously.[15]

Her letters to Greenslet concerning *My Ántonia* are filled with complaints about advertising, reviewing, stocking, and promotion. You are more committed to the fiction of Clara Louise Burnham than to mine, she complained to Greenslet, referring to a best-selling novelist whose formulaic novels pleased the popular taste. Her assumption that Houghton Mifflin failed to recognize her literary stature was not dispelled when Greenslet told her that *My Ántonia* might have significant sales as a children's book.[16]

Cather's dissatisfaction with her publisher was complicated by her friendly personal and professional relationship with her editor, whom she considered both connected to and separate from the organization he represented. In her letters of complaint she frequently referred to Houghton Mifflin in the third person, distinguishing the impersonal company from her personal bond with Greenslet, as if trying to imagine author and editor allied against an insensitive enemy. When she felt that Houghton Mifflin had not sufficiently supported and promoted *My Ántonia*, she asked Greenslet whether the Houghton Mifflin mind and heart might be fixed on a different sort of novel, the kind she did not want to write. Frankly, she said, she despaired of a future with them: "they" did not believe they could make much money on her, and they would also be careful not to lose much.[17]

Cather's growing belief in the literary power and commercial potential of her fiction led her after *My Ántonia* was published to abandon Greenslet and Houghton Mifflin for Alfred A. Knopf, who was just starting a new publishing company. In Knopf Cather found a man who believed that novels should be beautifully designed, aesthetically rich, and commercially successful. Her confidence was justified: throughout the 1920s and 1930s Cather's satisfaction with the appearance and marketing of her novels increased along with their sales and her royalties. *My Ántonia* had been published in 1918 in a first edition of only 3,500 copies. Cather earned only $1,300 in the first year of publication, $400 in the second. In September, 1922, by contrast, Knopf published *One of Ours* in an edition of 15,000 copies; 40,500 copies were in print by November. The following year Cather earned $19,000 in royalties.

Cather's decision to leave Houghton Mifflin for Knopf was undoubtedly the wisest professional decision she ever made. But her departure made it more difficult to protect and defend *My Ántonia*, since she could only rely on Greenslet's loyalty to a former author – not a strong counter to the publisher's desire to make money on a novel that sold increasingly well as Cather's literary reputation soared. For over twenty years Cather fought to keep Houghton Mifflin from turning *My Ántonia* into a paperback edition, an annotated student edition, a movie, a radio play

– all forms of distortion that Cather thought would cheapen and violate the integrity of her novel. Because she had drawn on so many early memories in creating her story, My Ántonia seemed part of Cather herself. She did not struggle in the same way to protect her first three novels, and in fact once, when Houghton Mifflin wanted to sell My Ántonia in a dollar paperback edition in a chain of drug stores, she sacrificed O Pioneers! instead, almost as if she were giving up one of her children to save her favorite.

In her correspondance with Greenslet, Cather always referred to My Ántonia as "she" rather than "it": her novel appears in these letters as a living, breathing woman, vulnerable to being cheapened – indeed, sexually exploited – by a crass publisher who views her as a commercial object. Writing Greenslet about his long campaign to turn My Ántonia into a paperback edition, an annotated student edition, and a film, she told him that he had never treated Ántonia gallantly: he was always trying to do her in and make her cheap by putting her into paperback. Ántonia had done well enough for Houghton Mifflin just as she was, Cather said, and did not need to be compromised in a cut-rate drugstore edition or chopped up and rewritten by some Houghton Mifflin employee for classroom use. A cut in the *text* was unthinkable, Cather said – how could Houghton Mifflin imagine reducing the whole book to some few thousand words for high school students? Such a dismemberment of books was a stupid, brutal trade, she told Greenslet – it was like sending writers through a meatpacking plant to be chopped up and packaged.[18]

This important letter suggests some of the psychological and emotional reasons why Cather struggled to retain My Ántonia's literary integrity, which she associated only with the illustrated hardback edition. My Ántonia is not only a book, but also a woman – embodying both the heroine and Cather herself. And the female body of this text is vulnerable to mutilation by the impersonal forces of the marketplace, represented here by Houghton Mifflin editors who want to dismember texts to increase sales. The text of Ántonia is also Cather the woman author trying to make her way in the world without being cheapened or compromised – economic imagery that also suggests sexual tainting.

Cather was not averse to gaining fame and making money: she just wanted to do so on her own terms, terms that defined herself as an artist and her novels as original, seamless expressions of an individual imagination. She was also quite willing to use the language of economics to bolster her arguments, as when she told Greenslet that it made no financial sense to sell Ántonia to a book club – that might boost sales temporarily, but diminish them in the long run. Better to keep the novel in hardback as a slow, steady, and dignified seller. Author and publisher possessed a good property, Cather told Greenslet – they should keep Ántonia to themselves.[19]

Cather's letters to Houghton Mifflin promoting and defending *My Ántonia* mix different, sometimes contradictory, strains of rhetoric: she uses the language of sexuality, of virginity, of aesthetics, of property, whatever was necessary to maintain control, knowing that Greenslet was trying to balance the roles of gentleman, appreciator of the arts, and businessman. Cather projected so much of herself into the novel – as well as her memories of Annie Pavelka – that she understandably thought of this text as a woman. But her imagining the novel as female also gave her a rhetorical strategy with her editor: she could influence Greenslet to treat Ántonia like a lady. In fighting off the Grant Wood illustrations, for example, she reminded Greenslet that Ántonia had gone her own way over the years, quietly and with dignity; now was no time for a fancy coming out party: it would be wrong to dress her up and push her forward. She and Greenslet had saved her Ántonia from textbooks, from dismemberment, from omnibuses: couldn't they now save her from colored illustrations? Greenslet would have had to have been a cad not to agree, and he did.[20]

It is possible to see Cather's efforts to limit access to *My Ántonia* as a form of elitism – hardback editions could only be purchased by people of a certain class and income. But from her perspective, she was trying both to prevent her novel's dismemberment and to preserve an author/reader bond based on sympathy rather than coercion. She did not want her work taught in high schools, for example, because she did not want students to grow up hating her. "When we find ourselves on shipboard, among hundreds of strangers," she wrote, "we very soon recognize those who are sympathetic to us. We like a writer much as we like individuals; for what he is, simply, underneath his accomplishments."[21] Reading, Cather believed, should be like striking up a friendship, neither coerced nor codified. Hence her opposition to book clubs, which turned books into selected, assigned friends. The one exception she made to her policy of preserving *My Ántonia's* dignity was in 1943, when she agreed to an armed services paperback edition.

Over the years, Cather won nearly all her battles with her first publisher over *My Ántonia*. Years after the deaths of both Cather and Greenslet, Houghton Mifflin continued to agree to keep Ántonia out of the movies because of what a 1970 memo termed a "gentleman's agreement" with Willa Cather.[22] So – as rebellious in challenging gender roles as she was in her life and art – Cather demanded that her publishers treat her novel as a lady, and eventually they did. Now, of course, the copyright on *My Ántonia* has expired, along with Houghton Mifflin's control, and the novel has appeared in several paperback editions as well as a made-for-TV movie.

* * * * *

Cather did not often make major changes between the first and second editions of her novels, but *My Ántonia* is an exception. The text of the 1918 version was reprinted unchanged until 1926, when Houghton Mifflin published a revised version from the first-edition plates. There were a few minor textual changes, but the major change was Cather's extensive revising and cutting of the Introduction, in which the author "Cather" describes her train journey with Jim Burden. Ferris Greenslet had convinced Cather that it made economic and artistic sense to publish a revised edition in 1926: a revision could be advertised as a new edition, unlike a simple reprint. He also had never liked the Introduction, which he thought made the emotional failures of Jim

Burden's adult life too explicit, and recommended that Cather eliminate it.

Cather had never been satisfied with the Introduction herself; it was the only part of the novel she had found laborious to write. She believed she needed an introduction, she told Greenslet, because the reader had to understand the unsuccesful personal life of the narrator to appreciate the later part of the novel. But she agreed with his criticisms, and decided to shorten it.[23] All editions of *My Ántonia* since then, with the exception of the Library of America edition, have used the revised 1926 version of the Introduction.

The original 1918 version of the Introduction gives us more information about Jim Burden's wife, the narrator's dislike for Mrs. Burden's superficial enthusiasms, and Jim's unhappy marrige. We also learn much more about Jim's role as an entrepreneurial capitalist who has helped to develop the West, raising money "for new enterprises in Wyoming or Montana" and helping young men do "remarkable things with mines and timber and oil." The 1918 Introduction hints that Jim's passionate energies, unsatisfied in a childless marriage with a flashy, cause-driven woman, might have been channeled into a search for hidden riches in the land: he likes to go "hunting for lost parks or exploring new canyons" that might yield their treasures, seeming to prefer the company of young men to that of his wife.[24]

The 1918 Introduction thus makes Jim a troubling narrator: to what extent might his urge to tell Ántonia's story betray a need to control feminine wealth and power, the same need he expresses when, in finding a sexualized landscape of "lost parks" and "new canyons," he turns these natural riches into capital? We see the connection between possession and storytelling in both versions when Jim changes the title of his story from "Ántonia" to "My Ántonia," the "my" suggesting both subjectivity and ownership, but this link is stronger in the 1918 Introduction.

In her revision, Cather also dramatically changes the relationship between the unnamed woman writer who narrates the Introduction and Jim Burden, her old friend who writes the novel. In the 1926 Introduction, the one used in all current paperback versions of the novel, Cather gives us a genderless narrator who may or may not be a writer – all we know is that this person grew up in Nebraska, was friendly with Jim Burden, meets him on a train, shares his memories of Ántonia, and agrees to read his manuscript. Jim is the only author of the 1926 version: " 'From time to time I've been writing down what I remember about Antonia,' he told me." Eventually he brings the manuscript to the narrator, and *My Ántonia* begins: thus we can assume that the novel we read is the one Jim Burden wrote.

In the 1918 version, by contrast, the narrator is a woman writer (assumed by most critics to be a version of Cather) who suggests that she and Jim *both* write down their memories of Ántonia: thus the creative spark for the story comes from her. But Jim finishes a manuscript, while the narrator confesses that hers "had not gone beyond a few straggling notes." She then presents Jim's manuscript to us "substantially as he brought it to me."[25] The word "substantially," removed from the 1926 version, of course changes our reading experience completely: the unnamed woman writer is thus an editor, and we have no way of knowing what changes she may have made in Jim's manuscript. So the "meaning" of the 1918 *My Ántonia* is doubly indeterminate, because we have both an unreliable narrator/writer (Jim) and an unreliable editor/writer ("Cather").

When she revised the 1918 Introduction, Cather clearly gave over to Jim the novel's creative inspiration, as well as its authorship. She may have decided that the double subjectivity of editor and writer was a needlessly complex narrative strategy, that her readers would find one unreliable narrator – Jim Burden – enough to cope with. And by having Jim already at work on Antonia's story when he meets "Cather" on the train, she gives far more inner need to his storytelling.

Because Jim Burden shares so much of Cather's biography, many critics have tended to assume that he speaks for her. Such an assumption is always problematic, because it makes too easy an equation between life and art, author and narrator. And when we consider that the two introductions to *My Ántonia* represent Jim's version of Ántonia as either murkily inaccessible (1918) or enthusiastically personal (1926), we need to be especially careful not to imagine that Jim is a simple mask for Willa Cather.

In both introductions, however, Cather underlines the subjectivity of his narrative – and of all narrative – by having Jim title his manuscript "My Ántonia." Storytelling, as the addition of "my" suggests, is both possessive and subjective. In telling the story from his own angle of vision, Jim necessarily gives us "his" Ántonia. Cather's first readers were not disturbed by this, but in the last ten years critics concerned with the politics of representation have noted that we are never given Ántonia's story. Her stories, her conversation, even her memories are filtered through Jim Burden's memory, imagination, and desire.

When Willa Cather published *My Ántonia* in 1918, the time was ripe for her to be recognized as a major American novelist. Her first novel, *Alexander's Bridge* (1912), had received polite but unenthusiastic reviews from critics, who noted her command of style along with her deference to Edith Wharton and Henry James. After Cather turned to her Nebraska past in *O Pioneers!* (1913) and *The Song of the Lark* (1915), she drew more favorable notice; reviewers saw emerging in her work an authentic American voice, one free of the stultifying accents of genteel culture and the lifeless clichés of popular fiction.

During this period important critics like H. L. Mencken – America's foremost man of letters and tastemaker – and Randolph Bourne hoped for a revitalized and indigenous American literature. They wanted writers who would displace the waning influence of New England literary culture and reflect the rising power of the Middle West; writers who would challenge middle-class pieties, as Sinclair Lewis later did in *Babbitt*; and writers who would establish an American literary culture separate from that of England. After the publication of *O Pioneers!* and *The Song of the Lark*, Mencken and Bourne had high hopes for Willa Cather. When they read *My Ántonia*, they found her promise fulfilled. Bourne praised Cather's breaking of "stiff moral molds" in *My Ántonia* and congratulated her for leaving the ranks of "provincial" writers and entering the world of "modern literary art." Meanwhile, delighted by the "extraordinary reality" and artistic command he found in the novel, Mencken became Cather's champion, anointing her in the pages of *Smart Set*, the influential cultural journal he edited.[26]

In the first major assessment of Cather in a literary history, *Contemporary American Novelists: 1900–1920* (1922), Carl Van Doren, the influential editor of the *Cambridge History of American Literature*, compared her favorably with her mentor Sarah Orne Jewett and praised the "rich vigor" of Cather's pioneer fiction, which he thought aligned her with Whitman. In *My Ántonia*, following so soon after *O Pioneers!* and *The Song of the Lark*, Van Doren found a promise for "future development that the work of but two or three other established American novelists holds out."[27] Throughout the 1920s Cather's literary reputation – and the sales of her books – continued to rise. She won the Pulitzer Prize for *One of Ours* (1922), then went on to publish *A Lost Lady* (1923), *The Professor's House* (1925), *My Mortal Enemy* (1926), and *Death Comes for the Archbishop* (1927).

My Ántonia did not receive additional critical attention until the 1930s and 1940s, when critical assessments of Cather's *oeuvre* began to appear in articles, reviews, and books. These were difficult decades for Cather's literary reputation. She began to anger a new generation of critics and reviewers who, influenced by the economic and social collapse of the Depression as well as by Marxist political thought, believed that art should grapple with the stern social, political, and economic realities of the time. The novels Cather published during the period – *Shadows on the Rock* (1931), *Lucy Gayheart* (1935), *Sapphira and the Slave Girl* (1940) – did not impress them. For critics enamored of *The Grapes of Wrath*, Cather's fiction seemed soft, romantic, escapist. Where was the struggle between the workers and the bosses? Where was the attack on capitalism?[28]

In his famous essay "The Case Against Willa Cather," Granville Hicks assigned Cather's literary decline to her growing political conservatism. Having surrendered to a "supine romanticism," Hicks charged, Cather could no longer describe "life as it is." Critics like Newton Arvin, Edmund Wilson, and Lionel Trilling agreed, finding Cather an increasingly nostalgic and escapist writer. Cather wrote, contended Newton Arvin in a typical commentary in the left-wing *New Republic*, as if the "struggle between the classes did not exist," and so failed to come to grips with the "real life of her time."[29] Unaware of how their own ideological positions were shaping their supposedly objective aesthetic views, such critics assumed they were recording – rather than creating – the decline of Cather's literary reputation.

While Cather's own literary status slipped as a result of such attacks, *My Ántonia*'s stature remained relatively unchallenged. Most of the left-wing critics thought the novel the highwater mark of her fiction, and even Granville Hicks, perhaps her most unsympathetic critic, located the beginning of Cather's literary decline after *My Ántonia*. But whereas to Cather's earlier reviewers *My Ántonia* seemed the beginning of a great career, to the critics of the 1930s and 1940s – their vision shaped by the politics of gender as well as class – it seemed to mark the last full expression of Cather's literary power. Such views helped shape even the critical assessment of a writer friendly to Cather and her work, Henry Seidel Canby, whose patronizing assessment of Cather in Robert Spiller's *Literary History of the United States* (1948) seemed to find her gender inconsistent with literary greatness. "Her art was not a big art," Canby concluded. "She is preservative, almost antiquarian, content with much space in little room – feminine in this, and in her passionate revelation of the values which conserve the life of the emotions."[30]

During the 1950s and 1960s, although *My Ántonia* did not attract extensive critical attention, it began to be reassessed by critics who respected Cather as a conscious artist. For the first time Cather's critics were exclusively scholars and academics, holding appointments in English departments, writing interpretations and analyses in articles intended for scholarly journals. Drawing on the critical discourse that dominated the academy during these years – the "New Criticism" – James E. Miller, Jr., found the much-valued trait of unity in *My Ántonia*, which juxtaposed, in his view, the cycles of nature with the cycles of human and societal life. Terence Martin, similarly influenced by the new critical directive to find "structural coherence" in a valued work, found Cather's unifying principle in Jim Burden's "drama of memory." From Miller's and Martin's new critical perspective, Cather was the conscious artist, in control of her materials, shap-

ing a narrator who also articulated her vision. "Her narrator, in
short, serves Miss Cather as the vehicle for her own quest for
meaning and value," Martin observes.[31] Other critics, influenced
by the new critical emphasis on form, genre, and literary allu-
sion, explored Cather's classical inheritance, linking *My Ántonia*
to the pastoral and the epic, reshaped in an American frontier
context.[32] In addition to finding *My Ántonia* a work of artistic
unity and integrity, such critics also praised the novel as an affirmative, celebratory narrative of the nation's agrarian past.

In 1971 Blanche Gelfant broke strongly from new critical perspectives in her important essay, "The Forgotten Reaping-Hook:
Sex in *My Ántonia*." Challenging the critical view that the novel
was a "splendid celebration of American frontier life" and Jim
Burden a reliable narrator, Gelfant argued that this "self-
deluded" character belonged to a "remarkable gallery of characters for whom Cather consistently invalidates sex." Jim Burden's
fear of mature sexuality shaped his story, Gelfant contended, and
the novel was marked by sexual disturbance, repression, and distortion. In her view, Cather had written neither an affirmative
nor a unified novel, but one "far more exciting – complex, subtle, aberrant."[33]

Gelfant did not directly address the issue of authorial inten-
tion, but at times she hinted that Jim's unconscious need to
shape a safe narrative – the safety of which was constantly be-
trayed by disturbing textual details – might also be Willa
Cather's. She spoke of the "strange involuted nature" of Cather's
avoidance of sexuality in her fiction, and argued that we should
value *My Ántonia* not only for its artistic power and historical
affirmation, but also for its "negations and evasions." Although
she did not explicitly address the author's "negations and evasions," Gelfant anticipated, by calling attention to textual ambiguities and anomalies, the direction Cather scholarship would
take in the 1970s and 1980s. Influenced by feminist theory and
cultural studies, scholars began to explore what *My Ántonia*
masked, transformed, displaced, repressed, and omitted.

Feminist criticism has focussed on questions of sexuality, gender, and representation. Although it had been a matter of literary
gossip and assumption that Willa Cather was a lesbian, it was not

until 1982 that Deborah Lambert made a direct connection between Cather's sexuality and her writing: "Cather was a lesbian who could not, or did not, acknowledge her homosexuality and who, in her fiction, transformed her emotional life and experiences into acceptable, heterosexual forms and guises." In her view, Cather could not write straightforwardly of her love for women in *My Ántonia*, and so created in Jim Burden a male mask for her own desire, and yet still could not "allow him full expression of her feelings." Jim could not simply love and marry Ántonia – the "homosexual threat" to Cather's disguise would have been too great.[34]

In "*My Ántonia*, Jim Burden, and the Dilemma of the Lesbian Writer," Judith Fetterley also finds Jim an unconvincing mask for a lesbian consciousness and argues for his "essential femaleness." Unlike Lambert, she discovers signs of Cather's resistance to this male masquerade in her portrayal of the sensual Lena Lingard, "one model of lesbian sexuality."[35]

In her essay "Displacing Homosexuality: The Use of Ethnicity in Willa Cather's *My Ántonia*," Katrina Irving agrees with Lambert's and Fetterley's argument that homosexuality enters *My Ántonia*, albeit in disguise. In her view, however, Cather's "mask" for homosexual desire is not Jim Burden but her loving portrayal of the hired girls. Irving contends that Cather displaced her ambivalence toward her lesbian identity onto the figure of the immigrant woman, an ethnic "other" who can stand in for the homosexual identity Cather could not directly name.[36]

In my article " 'The Thing Not Named': Willa Cather as a Lesbian Writer," and later in "Gender, Sexuality, and Point of View; Teaching *My Ántonia* from a Feminist Perspective," I argue that, although Cather could not draw directly on her love and desire for women, we should not assume that male characters are simply "masks" for a lesbian consciousness – to do that is to limit Cather's imagination, which allows her to invent characters different from herself. Nor should we assume that the overt heterosexual story is the false "cover" story, the hidden lesbian story the "real" one: such a vision also limits Cather's imaginative richness, and turns interpretation into a reductive process of decoding. Rather, we might think of meaning as multiple, shifting,

21

indeterminate, as the constant interplay of figure and ground, overt and covert, heterosexual and homosexual.[37]

Feminist critics of the novel who focus on issues of gender and representation disagree over the novel's challenge to patriarchal views of women depending on whether they cleanly separate Cather from Jim Burden's male-defined view or identify her with her narrator. In her discussion of *My Ántonia*, Susan Rosowski contends that Jim's representation of Antonia reveals "conventionally male attitudes": as he writes possessively about his Ántonia, imagining her as a mythic earth mother, Cather explores the ways in which the culture assigns to men the position of perceiving and recording subject, to women the position of object. But Cather disrupts Jim's patriarchal narrative, Rosowski argues, by showing us that Ántonia herself is a storyteller, and by letting her break through the myths that Jim tries to impose.[38] Working with the Benda illustrations, Jean Schwind similarly deconstructs Jim's narrative, arguing that Cather uses the realistic woodcuts to undermine Jim's romanticism and to challenge his complacent, and limited, view of Ántonia as a generative female archetype. Ann Romines, by contrast, does not think that Cather distinguishes herself from Jim's celebratory view: in fact, Romines argues, she endorses it, and so reflects rather than challenges patriarchal views of women. In the last pages of the novel, she writes, "Jim and Cather seem co-conspirators in the mythologizing of Ántonia."[39]

While Rosowski's, Schwind's, and Romines's feminist approaches to *My Ántonia* see Cather as a female voice either resisting or perpetuating oppressive, romanticized narratives of gender, critics drawing on new historicist and cultural studies approaches – which often call our attention to gaps or absences in the text – point out the ways in which *My Ántonia* perpetuates silencing narratives of peoples Cather imagined as Other. A product of her historical moment, Cather revised some of her culture's dominant stories but could not help perpetuating others, particularly in the context of race and ethnicity.

Mike Fischer sees *My Ántonia* as a story of origins written "for whites only." By portraying the Nebraska landscape as unsettled and ripe for cultivation, the novel erases the Native American presence which in fact antedated white settlement in Nebraska, much as the whites had erased the Native Americans by appropriating their land, removing them to reservations, and then forgetting their existence. "There can be no Eden in Nebraska," he concludes, "because its origins are not innocent." In celebrating the West of settlement and European immigration, Cather is blinded to the effects of immigration on the West's indigenous populations. Hence, in telling some of the untold stories in American culture in *My Ántonia*, Cather inevitably silences others.[40]

But Richard Millington, who places *My Ántonia* in the context of oral storytelling and folktale rather than the sociopolitical (and now literary) categories of race, class, and gender, finds a far more subversive and radical novel than does Fischer. In *My Ántonia*, by celebrating the power of storytelling to give meaning to experience, Millington argues, Cather challenges the bourgeois genre of the novel and the social conventions the novel inevitably reflects (such as connecting emotional maturity with marriage and work rather than with dreaming, reverie or narrative flair). So, in Millington's view, Jim's return to Ántonia at the novel's end does not mark regression or romanticism, but "the defeat of the novel . . . by the story."[41]

* * * * *

Although most of Cather's critics and reviewers write convincingly as if they possessed the key to *My Ántonia*, when we place all these accounts together, noting that some are jarringly inconsistent and all are different, we can see how the criticism of *My Ántonia* upholds one of the insights of postmodern literary theory – that meaning is indeterminant. Of course all novels produce a variety of readings, depending on the historical and institutional circumstances in which the text is read, but *My Ántonia* has been particularly open to contradictory readings because of its complex and ambiguous narrative structure. Does Jim Burden speak for Willa Cather? Does Cather carefully maintain ironic distance from his vision? Or does she waver, at times detaching herself from Jim, at times seemingly identified with his perspective? The critics do not agree. In addition, Cather's critics disagree about whether the author of *My Ántonia* is a conscious artist, consummately in control of her aesthetic design, or whether her own unconscious desires and displacements – often surrounding sexuality – undermine *My Ántonia*'s narrative certainty. Contradictory readings of the novel seem to come with the territory.

Legitimately reflecting and exploring these differences, the readings of *My Ántonia* that follow take varied approaches to the novel. Drawing on recent developments in literary theory, the authors illuminate both the novel and the theoretical methods they employ, giving us not only new ways of thinking about *My Ántonia* but also questions to ask about other American novels.

In his essay placing Cather in the American literary tradition of Hawthorne, Twain, and Jewett, Miles Orvell challenges the romantic myth of literary originality that Cather herself encouraged. Reminding us that writers and texts are bound up in a web of literary and cultural influence, he places Cather in the context of inheritance and revision. Feminist scholars have tended to stress literary inheritance in connecting women writers to their foremothers, and revision (or re-vision) in exploring how women writers challenge and rewrite the male-authored texts of their forefathers. By showing how Willa Cather drew on both male and female literary traditions – inheriting and revising both – Orvell resists the assumption that gender is the only variable in determining a woman writer's complex relationship to her literary past. Simultaneously, he reminds us that women writers can, and do, influence the male writers who arrive later, suggesting that Cather's acceptance of time and change in *My Ántonia* prefigures the response of modernist writers like Fitzgerald, Faulkner, and Hemingway.

Willa Cather enjoyed placing herself in the company of Hawthorne, Twain, and Jewett when she wrote the preface to Jewett's *The Country of the Pointed Firs* – an elite literary grouping that only added to Cather's stature as a major writer. And she enjoyed attributing some sources of *My Ántonia* to folk culture, the stories she heard about immigrant lives after she moved to Nebraska. But one shaping influence she did not want to acknowledge, as Elizabeth Ammons' essay explains: her novel's indebtedness to African American music.

Reminding us that Cather was surrounded by black song and music in her Virginia childhood and familiar with the itinerant black piano players Blind Boone and Blind Tom, Ammons argues that Cather's debt to African American art – reflected primarily in the novel's nonlinear form – is repressed in the novel, erupting only in the portrayal of Blind d'Arnault, the black musician who entrances white Red Cloud with his sensual artistic power. Ammons squarely faces Cather's racism, evident in her stereotypic representation of d'Arnault as a black Other, yet simultaneously sees the pianist as the novel's creative genius. She expands our ways of thinking about literary influence, reminding us that writers can be shaped by such "low" art forms as popular music, and that white writers draw on black culture – even when (and maybe especially when) they do not acknowledge such inspiration openly.

Even while Cather was suppressing her debt to black culture in *My Ántonia*, she was separating herself from white Southern literary culture because she did not want to be known as a Southern novelist – an unprestigious, limiting literary classification in 1918. In her exploration of *My Ántonia*'s hidden and displaced Southernness, Ann Jones revivifies and enriches the category of regionalism, a category once used to define, and frequently to dismiss, women writers. In doing so, she suggests that region can be repressed in a narrative and become a troubling subtext. Like Willa Cather, Jim Burden grows up Virginia and moves to Nebraska, yet his Southern past is not openly represented, mourned, or acknowledged in *My Ántonia* – perhaps because in her own mind the author's childhood home was connected with a racially and sexually oppressive history. Like Ammons, Jones finds the return of the repressed in Cather's novel: Jim's Southern past refuses to stay buried, surfacing in the narrator's projections and displacements. And so, Jones suggests, a novel ostensibly concerned with one region or landscape may betray the ghostly traces of another. By exposing these traces, Jones offers us new, subtle ways to think about Cather, *My Ántonia*, and region.

In her reading of *My Ántonia* from a feminist perspective, Marilee Lindemann is also concerned with what is silenced in *My Ántonia* and what is given voice. Reminding us that Ántonia is a "figure" to Cather and Jim Burden, rather than a character, she sees *My Ántonia* as a novel primarily concerned with power and representation. Because he writes and tells the story, Jim Burden gets to say what the figure of Ántonia means, and Cather, in Lindemann's view, does not develop a strong counter-narrative that would dislodge or discredit Jim's story, which effectively silences Ántonia. Pointing out that women's voices are muted or relegated to the margins of the text, Lindemann argues that *My Ántonia* reflects Cather's skepticism about women's ability to compete with men in the contest of representation. The novel's feminism – which is not self-conscious – rests in Lindemann's view not in portrayals of hardy pioneer women, but in its bleak, unflinching recognition of women's lack of cultural and narrative authority.

* * * * *

A novel as rich as *My Ántonia* can be read many times, and each reading can be a different journey. Some strands in the narrative may stand out at one time, others another. The essays that follow direct our attention to different strands in Cather's design that will enrich our readings of *My Ántonia*, but ultimately the novel is created in us; we are the final storytellers. As we read, we enter into imaginative spaces opened for us by Willa Cather's words and by these essays, and so share in the creative process.

NOTES

1. Elizabeth Shepley Sergeant, *Willa Cather: A Memoir* (Lincoln: University of Nebraska Press, 1963), p. 107.
2. "Miss Jewett," in *Not Under Forty* (New York: Alfred A. Knopf, 1936), p. 91.
3. "Preface" to *Alexander's Bridge* (Boston: Houghton Mifflin, 1922), p. ix.
4. The dedication is quoted from the unpaginated dedication page of

My Ántonia (Boston: Houghton Mifflin, 1918; revised, 1926). Future page references in the text are to the 1926 edition. The phrase "hired girl" is adapted from Cather's title for Book II, "The Hired Girls."

5. *Willa Cather On Writing* (New York: Alfred A. Knopf, 1949), p. 94.
6. *The World and the Parish: Willa Cather's Articles and Reviews, 1893–1902*, ed. William Curtin (Lincoln: University of Nebraska Press, 1970), Volume I, p. 362.
7. "Preface," *Alexander's Bridge* (1922), p. vii.
8. Edith Lewis, *Willa Cather Living* (New York: Alfred A. Knopf, 1953), p. 31.
9. *The Kingdom of Art: Willa Cather's First Principles and Critical Statements 1893–1896*, ed. Bernice Slote (Lincoln: University of Nebraska Press, 1966), p. 448.
10. *Lincoln State Journal*, November 2, 1921, p. 7.
11. Sergeant, *Willa Cather: A Memoir*, p. 140.
12. Lewis, *Willa Cather Living*, p. 104.
13. Ferris Greenslet to Willa Cather, January 4, 1921, Houghton Mifflin correspondence, Houghton Library, Harvard University. According to Cather's will, her letters are not to be quoted directly.
14. Willa Cather to Mr. Scaife, March 13, 1917, April 7, 1917, and December 1917; Willa Cather to Ferris Greenslet, July 17, 1917 and November 24, 1917, Houghton Mifflin correspondence, Houghton Library, Harvard University, Cambridge, Massachusetts.
15. In "The Benda Illustrations to *My Ántonia*," Jean Schwind gives a full history of Cather's battles with Houghton Mifflin and argues that Benda's sketches provide a realistic counterpoint to Burden's romantic vision of Ántonia and Nebraska (*PMLA* 100 [January 1985]: 51–67).
16. Ferris Greenslet to Willa Cather, October 22, 1918, Houghton Mifflin correspondence, Houghton Library, Harvard University.
17. Willa Cather to Ferris Greenslet, May 19, 1919, Houghton Mifflin correspondence, Houghton Library, Harvard University.
18. Willa Cather to Ferris Greenslet [undated], Houghton Mifflin collection, Houghton Library, Harvard University.
19. Willa Cather to Ferris Greenslet, February 16, 1942, Houghton Mifflin correspondence, Houghton Library, Harvard University.
20. Willa Cather to Ferris Greenslet, January 29, 1938, Houghton Mifflin correspondence, Houghton Library, Harvard University.
21. "Miss Jewett," *Not Under Forty*, p. 94.

22. Interoffice memo of February 7, 1970, Houghton Mifflin correspondence, Houghton Library, Harvard University.

23. Willa Cather to Ferris Greenslet, February 15, 1926, Houghton Mifflin correspondence, Houghton Library, Harvard University.

24. Willa Cather, *My Ántonia* (New York: Literary Classics of the United States, 1987), p. 712.

25. *My Ántonia* (New York: Literary Classics of the United States), pp. 713–14.

26. Randolph Bourne, [Review of *My Ántonia*], *Critical Essays on Willa Cather*, ed. John J. Murphy (Boston: G. K. Hall, 1984), pp. 145–6; H. L. Mencken, [Review of *My Ántonia*], *Willa Cather and Her Critics*, ed. James Schroeter (Ithaca: Cornell University Press, 1967), p. 8.

27. Carl Van Doren, "Willa Cather," in *Willa Cather and Her Critics*, pp. 13–19.

28. For a fuller discussion of the politics of Cather's literary reputation, see my own article "Becoming Noncanonical: The Case Against Willa Cather," in *Reading in America: Literature and Social History*, ed. Cathy N. Davidson (Baltimore: Johns Hopkins University Press, 1989), pp. 240–258.

29. Granville Hicks, "The Case Against Willa Cather," in Schroeter, ed., pp. 139–147; Newton Arvin, "Quebec, Nebraska, and Pittsburgh," *New Republic* (August 12, 1931), p. 345.

30. *Literary History of the United States*, Volume 2, ed. Robert E. Spiller et al. (New York: 1948), p. 1216.

31. James E. Miller, Jr., "*My Ántonia*: A Frontier Drama of Time," *American Quarterly* 10 (1958): 476–84; Terence Martin, "The Drama of Memory in *My Ántonia*," *PMLA* 84 (1969): 304–11.

32. Paul A. Olsen, "The Epic and Great Plains Literature: Rolvaag, Cather and Neihardt," *Prairie Schooner* (1981): 263–85; David Stouck, *Willa Cather's Imagination* (Lincoln, 1975); Curtis Dahl, "An American Georgic: Willa Cather's *My Ántonia*," *Comparative Literature* 7 (1955): 43–51.

33. Blanche H. Gelfant, "The Forgotten Reaping-Hook: Sex in *My Ántonia*," *American Literature* 43 (1971): 60–82.

34. Deborah Lambert, "The Defeat of a Hero: Autonomy and Sexuality in *My Ántonia*," *American Literature* 53 (1982): 76–90.

35. Judith Fetterley, "*My Ántonia*, Jim Burden, and the Dilemma of the Lesbian Writer" in *Lesbian Texts and Contexts*, ed. Karla Jay and Joanne Glasgow (New York, 1990), pp. 145–163.

36. Katrina Irving, "Displacing Homosexuality: The Use of Ethnicity in

Willa Cather's *My Ántonia,'' Modern Fiction Studies* 36, no. 1 (Spring 1990): 91–102.

37. Sharon O'Brien, " 'The Thing Not Named': Willa Cather as a Lesbian Writer,'' *Signs: Journal of Women in Culture and Society* 9 (1984): 576–99, and "Gender, Sexuality, and Point of View: Teaching *My Ántonia* from a Feminist Perspective,'' *Approaches to Teaching Cather's My Ántonia,* ed. Susan Rosowski (New York: Modern Language Association, 1989), pp. 141–145.

38. Susan J. Rosowski, *The Voyage Perilous: Willa Cather's Romanticism* (Lincoln: University of Nebraska Press, 1986), pp. 75–94.

39. Schwind, "The Benda Illustrations,'' and Ann Romines, "After the Christmas Tree: Cather and Domestic Ritual,'' *American Literature* 60 (March 1988): 61–82.

40. Mike Fischer, "Pastoralism and Its Discontents: Willa Cather and the Burden of Imperialism,'' *Mosaic: A Journal for the Interdisciplinary Study of Literature* 23 (Winter 1990): 31–44.

41. Richard H. Millington, "Willa Cather and 'The Storyteller': Hostility to the Novel in *My Ántonia,'' American Literature* 66 (December 1994): 689–718.

2

Time, Change, and the Burden of Revision in *My Ántonia*

MILES ORVELL

IT'S easy to assume, when reading powerful works of fiction, that they come to us solely through an act of original creation and that genius is, precisely, the power of original authorship. Yet authorship is also the product of innumerable forces working upon the individual writer. And it takes nothing away from Willa Cather, or any other writer, to see them in the context of a field of influence, as inheritors of modes of formal articulation and of psychologies of experience. Indeed, as we begin to read works of fiction as part of an institution of literature, we see them even more richly than we might if taken as works of isolated genius. The patterns of innovation emerge even more sharply. *My Ántonia* is a work that is especially interesting to consider in this context, for it complexly negotiates its literary ancestry in a variety of ways, taking inspiration from the field of existing work at the same time that it revises, criticizes, and in many ways goes beyond its predecessors.

Willa Cather was herself acutely aware of her literary inheritance and on one occasion – a few years after the publication of *My Ántonia* (1918) – formulated an abbreviated canon, a list of great American fiction that may be seen as establishing a lineage for her own work. Introducing, in 1925, the Houghton Mifflin collection of stories by Sarah Orne Jewett, Cather included a summation that deliberately does honor to her subject but also tells us a good deal about herself: "If I were asked to name three American books which have the possibility of a long, long life, I would say at once, 'The Scarlet Letter,' 'Huckleberry Finn,' and 'The Country of the Pointed Firs.' I can think of no others that confront time and change so serenely."[1] There is much to ponder in this, not least the very inclusion of Jewett's *Pointed Firs* in such a triumvirate. Cather's estimation was not only an effort to boost Jewett's reputation at a moment when the latter's works were generally neglected, but an acknowledgment of Jewett's importance to an earlier generation of readers, including Willa Cather, who had read *The Country of the Pointed Firs* – along with the other stories Jewett had published in *Harper's, The Century*, and *The Atlantic* – with great admiration. If Henry James is missing from this list, it may reflect the fact that in Cather's case at least, James – a major early influence on her work – had been supplanted by Jewett. In any event, one couldn't easily acknowledge the transatlantic James *and* the adamantly local Jewett in the same breath, especially in the context of an encomium to works that "confront time and change" with serenity: for James's characters more often confront change with quiet anguish or tragic resignation.

There is, besides, something resolutely "American" in the geography of Cather's canonical gesture, and the transatlantic James would seem the odd man out in this company. All three of her authors were working to construct a literature that exploited regional characteristics and the complex social character of American life in a way that Cather herself would carry forward. It is tempting also to read this list as a record of Cather's indebtedness to the formal and psychological structures already worked out by Hawthorne, Twain, and Jewett. For in many ways Cather borrowed from all three earlier writers and created in *My Ántonia* a work that pays tribute to the past at the same time that it seriously revises the work of her predecessors.

Like Hawthorne in *The Scarlet Letter*, Cather presents herself initially in the guise of an editor, a mediator between a story and an audience. "Last summer," she begins, "in a season of intense heat, Jim Burden and I happened to be crossing Iowa on the same train. He and I are old friends, we grew up together in the same Nebraska town, and we had a great deal to say to each other."[2] And she goes on to describe her conversation with Jim about their mutual friend Ántonia, and their determination each to write narratives about her. But only Jim completes his, and the story we read, printed in four "books," is Jim Burden's.

(Cather pretends to have done just a little tinkering with it in the first version of the Introduction [1918], which concludes: "My own story was never written, but the following narrative is Jim's manuscript, substantially as he brought it to me.")[3] Who is this friend, now living in New York and apparently well connected in the literary world, who accepts the burden of handling the manuscript for the novice author? We could complicate matters by positing a nameless, ungendered fictional persona – for the Introduction really gives us no clues to the identity of the editor. But let's agree that most people reading the book will assume that the "editor" is Cather (or "Cather," to separate further the real author from her authorial persona). The author thus stands before us, somewhat ambiguously, as a presenter, an editor, a translator of an existing manuscript.

Just so Hawthorne had begun *The Scarlet Letter*, addressing the reader in the first person (though in a tone more jocular than Cather's) as the conveyor of a little roll of manuscript that was found along with, and explains, the otherwise enigmatic piece of cloth – the scarlet letter itself – which Hawthorne had come upon simultaneously. But Hawthorne also makes clear that he has dressed up the original six pages – "written" by Mr. Surveyor Pue – and that the imagining of the "motives and modes of passion that influence the characters who figure in it" are his own responsibility.[4] Thus Hawthorne's "Custom-House" Preface – a longer and richer document than Cather's Introduction – serves to authenticate the story of Hester Prynne that will follow; but it also serves notice that the teller of the tale, author Hawthorne, will be embroidering upon, and embellishing, the original tale.

Cather conceived her own function as "editor" or "presenter" in a different way, making little or no acknowledgment of any alterations in Jim's narrative. But then why use the framing device at all? Borrowing an effect from Hawthorne, Cather's frame does enhance the authenticity of Jim's story, granting it a kind of existence apart from the storyteller. But where Hawthorne uses the frame to excuse a heightened artistry that will follow, Cather uses hers to disarm our expectations of "art," offering instead a narrative that promises to be the real thing itself, an authentic narrative of Ántonia by someone who knew her and is, for reasons we may never fully understand, obsessed with her. (To Ferris Greenslet, Cather's editor at Houghton Mifflin, the manuscript carried "the most thrilling shock of recognition of the real thing of any" he'd ever read.)[5]

Because *My Ántonia* is presented as a narrative written by someone who is not a "writer," we may grant it a freedom from the requirements of the well made story, a seeming roughness at the edges and seams. If we find sections that seem filled with a kind of symbolic energy not fully absorbed into a finished system of narrative meaning – the killing of the snake by Jim; Wick Cutter's sexual "mistake"; Jim's dream of Lena advancing with a reaping hook; the story of the bride thrown to the wolves – we can accept them as chunks of "reality" that lend even greater authenticity to the story. And we can accept a homeliness in the diction and metaphor that adds to the authorial voice a quality of vernacular experience: "All day the storm went on," Jim reports. "The snow did not fall this time, it simply spilled out of heaven, like thousands of feather-beds being emptied" (105). Yet all of this artlessness is, of course, part of Cather's greater art, and her master here is Mark Twain, whose own masterpiece, *Huckleberry Finn*, is the second work named by Cather in her improvised canon.

Like Huck, Jim is an orphan at the outset of the story, though Jim's grandparents will create the haven in the storm that Huck never had. And Cather's assumption of Jim Burden's voice – admittedly a far more educated, more literary voice than Huck's – sometimes carries with it the qualities of concrete sensory observation that Twain discovered in Huck's sensibility: "As I looked about me I felt that the grass was the country, as the water is the sea," Jim recalls early in the book. "The red of the grass made all the great prairie the color of wine-stains, or of certain seaweeds when they are first washed up. And there was so much motion in it; the whole country seemed, somehow, to be running" (16). (Cf. *Huckleberry Finn*: "The river looked miles and miles across. The moon was so bright I could a counted the drift logs that went a slipping along, black and still, hundred yards out from shore. Everything was dead quiet, and it looked late, and *smelt* late. You know what I mean – I don't know the words to put it in." [Chapter VII]) Cather, like Twain, is making a virtue out of the seeming naivetë of her narrator, exploiting the resources of the vernacular, opposing her narrator's artlessness and the presumed artificiality of the "editor."

Moreover, in her characterization of Ántonia, Cather was dealing with a problem analogous to Twain's in his characterization of Jim. Both were constructing representations of a social class generally held in contempt by the dominant social group – the slave in antebellum Missouri, the immigrant in Nebraska. (We must remember that the prevailing prejudices tended to stigmatize ethnic minorities, encouraging them to erase their distinctive heritages in favor of "Americanization" – an assimilation into the English-speaking cultural mainstream.) The relationship between Jim Burden and Ántonia is surely not as daringly conceived as that between a white boy and a Negro slave in the antebellum South, but it does cross accepted social lines. Ántonia is an uneducated immigrant, Jim is a member of the "ruling class." Their childhood friendship doesn't strain credulity, for the breaking of taboos is easily permitted to children; but in sustaining their rapport over many years, Cather intends a deliberate contrast between two characters who thus manage to transcend in their relationship the barriers that customarily separate social classes in the United States: after all, Cather could have given Jim a more modest career than "legal counsel for one of the great Western railways" (x), with its enormously greater social power relative to Ántonia.

Cather's Ántonia resembles Twain's Jim in another significant way as well: like the nineteenth-century person of color, the immigrant in the twentieth century has often been considered a kind of primitive, closer to "natural" life than her "civilized" counterpart, more in touch with the earth, the seasons, the forces of regeneration, more relaxed with the human body itself. Burden reports, on his last visit to Ántonia, that as the Cuzaks looked at the family photographs "they leaned this way and that, and were not afraid to touch each other" (394). Like Twain's Jim, Cather's Ántonia seems imbued with a gift of empathy for all living things that operates like a touchstone in the novel, and her prolific offspring create a standard against which to measure

Jim's urban career and his sterile marriage. Much has been said about Cather's celebration of immigrants and their pioneer spirit, and especially her appreciation of the immigrant women of the frontier. Yet we should bear in mind that Cather's esteem for the rural Midwestern immigrant does not carry over to immigrants of the Eastern cities. The broken English of Ántonia is offered without any sense of authorial opprobrium: Ántonia exclaims, after Jim has killed the famous snake, "O Jimmy, he not bite you? You sure? Why you not run when I say?" (51) And at the end of the book, though her speech has greatly "improved," she is still given to say, of Jake and Otto, who made Mr. Shimerda's coffin, "Wasn't they good fellows, Jim?" (395) Ántonia's speech is not grammatically perfect, but it is functional and expressive. By contrast, Cather has nothing but scorn for the acquired English of the urban immigrant. In this passage from a 1936 essay on Jewett, Cather is trying to explain why the younger generation apparently find little of interest in Jewett's writings: "This hypothetical young man [i.e. the new reader] is perhaps of foreign descent: German, Jewish, Scandinavian. To him English is merely a means of making himself understood, of communicating his ideas. He may write and speak American English correctly, but only as an American may learn to speak French correctly. It is a surface speech: he clicks the words out as a bank clerk clicks out silver when you ask for change. For him the language has no emotional roots."[6] Sounding like Henry James here (in *The American Scene*), Cather's xenophobia and ethnic stereotyping has a lack of generosity wholly at odds with the generous vision of *My Ántonia*.

What was the difference between the immigrants Cather evidently scorned and those she loved? One factor surely was that the immigrant who "clicks the words out as a bank clerk" provokes Cather's hostility toward urban life generally and all that it embodies of a commercial civilization. The Shimerdas and others on the great plains are making their peace, if not their fortune, with nature: a feeling for the earth – a struggle with nature – possesses them as much as it does Cather. Cather had, it's clear, a Jeffersonian view of cities – "sores upon the body politic" –

which seemed to grow stronger as she grew older. Whatever cultural allure the city had in her earlier fiction was gradually replaced by a sense of urban depravity and treachery associated with immigrant life, a feeling that comes through with especial strength in her "sequel" to *My Ántonia*, the short story "Neighbour Rosicky."[7]

But Cather's sense of the land as a moral and aesthetic construction was not only a reaction against modern urban life; it derived in a more positive sense from her own experience growing up in Nebraska, and from the ultimate acceptance of that experience as the foundation for her art. And if *My Ántonia* represents the culmination of this repossession of her own creative source, then a key figure in arriving at that moment – and here we come to the third luminary in the Cather American canon – was Sarah Orne Jewett. We know how crucial to Willa Cather's development was Jewett, both as writer and as friend. Cather was generous in acknowledging her debt to the older writer on many occasions, and their relationship has been illuminated in detail by Sharon O'Brien.[8] What has not been fully explored, however, is the extent to which *My Ántonia* constitutes a kind of revision of Jewett's masterpiece, *The Country of the Pointed Firs*.

* * * * *

But let me first briefly recapitulate the Cather debt to Jewett. Cather spelled out at least one aspect of the debt in a 1913 interview printed in the *Philadelphia Record*, where she ranks Jewett with James and Twain as her favorite American authors and reveals the personal significance of the relationship, citing Jewett's opinion about Cather's early work, delivered to the aspiring writer when they met. (Cather and Jewett were personal friends only briefly [1908–1909] before the latter died.) "Write it as it is, don't try to make it like this or that. You can't do it in anybody else's way – you will have to make a way of your own."[9] In effect, Jewett was giving Cather – who had previously modeled herself on Henry James – license to claim as her own aesthetic province the fascinating stories of her childhood, stories that she heard from the neighboring Scandinavian and Bohemian immigrant women especially, who talked to her about their lives in the old country and the new.[10]

In other ways as well Cather would use Jewett as a vehicle for her own aesthetic theories: Jewett's stories, Cather wrote in introducing her work in 1925, were "not stories at all, but life itself," a trope that derives from the rhetoric of late nineteenth-century realism. But in other respects, Jewett's fiction, emerging out of the local color tradition, was at odds with the more sensationalistic urban realism of the 1890s that laid the foundation for the tradition of naturalism in modern literature. Cather, identifying herself with the female world of Jewett and with her rural traditions, would celebrate in Jewett what the two shared, seeing in the older writer a model for a kind of writing that would claim both the importance of regional specificity and the sophistication of an art that was "timeless." With Jewett, Cather wrote, the "magnitude of the subject-matter is not of primary importance"; an "idyl of Theocritus, concerned with sheep and goats and shade and pastures, is to-day as much alive as the most dramatic passages of the Iliad" (Preface, 7).[11]

The aesthetic of pastoral simplicity, of the "natural," that Cather builds upon Jewett's art is posited in contrast to an aesthetic of decoration, in which the artist is "improving upon his subject-matter, by using his 'imagination' upon it and twisting it to suit his purpose," an aesthetic of the "brilliant sham," of "costumed" fiction, that Cather associates with the painter's stilted studio poses. Against this overdecorated, overstuffed aesthetic (Cather had earlier elaborated her ideas in a 1922 essay called "The Novel Demeublée" – i.e., unfurnished),[12] Cather defines an art of organic functionalism that in many ways unites Jewett (and Cather herself, by implication) to the modernist project of the 1920s. Borrowing a pair of contrasting terms from Gilbert Murray, Cather describes the difference between the beauty of ornamentation, "gorgeously gilded and painted," and the quite different beauty of "a modern yacht, where there is no ornamentation at all; our whole sensation of pleasure in watching a yacht under sail comes from the fact that every line of the craft is designed for one purpose, that everything about it furthers that

purpose, so that it has an organic, living simplicity and direct-
ness" (Preface, 11). The metaphor of the yacht embodies a whole
constellation of aesthetic and moral values – the simplicity and
honesty of functional design, an art free of corrupting decorative
embellishment – that writers of the twenties were invoking as
they positioned themselves against the last hollow remnants of
sentimental, genteel fiction.[13]

Representing Jewett as an "organic" artist, Cather was re-
claiming a female counterpart of the "usable past" that Van
Wyck Brooks, Lewis Mumford, and others were looking for in
the teens and twenties and finding in such nineteenth-century
male writers as Emerson, Thoreau, and Whitman. In thus "mod-
ernizing" Jewett, Cather was rescuing her mentor from the
oblivion of seeming "old-fashioned"; but she was also naming
qualities in her own work that marked her change from a writer
in an older, more elaborately detailed and embellished nineteenth-century mode to a writer of a simplified, artlessly functional prose. (Cather would reiterate these values when she
wrote *The Professor's House* – published in the same year as the
Jewett preface.)[14] If Cather had started out as a nineteenth-
century writer (cf. *The Song of the Lark*), she was ending up a
modernist; and Jewett had served as a kind of bridge in making
the transition.

But Cather's preference for a functionalist aesthetic should not
lead us to underestimate the importance of the "imagination" in
her work. The concept is central to her theory of fiction and to
the conception of *My Ántonia*. Again, Jewett is a catalyst for
Cather, who begins her introduction to Jewett's stories with an
observation found in a package of Jewett's letters: "The thing
that teases the mind over and over for years," Jewett had written, "and at last gets itself put down rightly on paper – whether
little or great, it belongs to Literature." And Cather adds, in her
own voice: "The shapes and scenes that have 'teased' the mind
for years, when they do at last get themselves rightly put down,
make a very much higher order of writing, and a much more
costly, than the most vivid and vigorous transfer of immediate
impressions" (Preface, 6). Rather than a direct transcript of incident or sensation (cf. Hemingway's effort to capture the exact

feel of passing emotions), Cather is formulating here a theory of the imagination that links her with the more meditative side of Wordsworth, in which the poet's steeped recollection of past events and characters eventually issues forth in a deeply felt lyrical utterance. Notice the terms in which Jim Burden's story is presented by Cather: as the editor and Burden sit chatting on the train crossing Iowa, "our talk kept returning to a central figure, a Bohemian girl whom we had both known long ago. More than any other person we remembered, this girl seemed to mean to us the country, the conditions, the whole adventure of our childhood. . . . [Jim's] mind was full of her that day. He made me see her again, feel her presence, revived all my old affection for her" (xi). And, it turns out, Jim has been writing down his memories of Ántonia on his trips across the country, a process which concludes with his putting the finished manuscript – which is what we will read – into the hands of the editor.

* * * * *

We recall that Cather had singled out, in the 1925 preface to the Jewett volume, a quality shared by all three of her nominated classics – *The Scarlet Letter, Huckleberry Finn,* and *The Country of the Pointed Firs:* "I can think of no others that confront time and change so serenely." And it is here precisely that Cather's *My Ántonia* constitutes such a significant "revision" of Jewett's earlier book. Revision always connotes a somewhat ambiguous relationship: what is being revised is still there, but the original has been rewritten, reformulated, revised. And in this context, allowing for the many gross differences between the two texts, what may be most interesting to examine are those points where the resemblance seems strongest. Looking at a work of fiction in this way implies a conception of literature not as a straight line of "progress," but rather as a complex process of circling around and back to earlier works, which in various ways influence later works. From this perspective, all literary creations have ancestors and effect revisions. It seems especially important to unravel these connections in the case of a writer like Willa Cather, for whom the discovery of her individual voice was an act of deliberate and self-conscious invention, yet one founded closely on the example of others, especially Jewett.

The most obvious point of contact between *My Ántonia* and *Pointed Firs* is the essential narrative structure used to present their fictional communities, for in each case we find a "visitor" serving as the main point of view, the narrator through whose eyes we see and understand the other characters. In Jewett's work, the narrator is returning to a small town called Dunnet's Landing, off the coast of Maine, which she had fallen in love with while on a brief visit a few summers before. She is spending the summer in the town, and she soon finds herself involved – as a friendly observer – in the lives of the townspeople, especially her landlady, Mrs. Todd. After a series of stories, each of which centers on a single, usually somewhat eccentric character, the narrator returns to the city, her permanent home.

Cather's narrator, Jim Burden, constructs his own narrative around the few return visits he makes to the Nebraska farming community near Black Hawk; but unlike Jewett's summertime visitor, Jim has grown up there. And while a number of characters populate his story, the narrator's main interest remains focused on Ántonia, who arrives in the community with Jim and who remains there for most of her life. Jim, on the other hand, leaves to go to college and establishes his life and career outside the community. He returns, however, at intervals, and *My Ántonia* is the story of his growing up and the story of his returns. At the end of the work, as with *Pointed Firs*, the narrator is about to leave the community.

One obvious difference between these two revenants is that of gender. Jewett, using a female visitor, creates a series of linked stories in which her narrator grows progressively closer to the community and to Mrs. Todd. In establishing a community in which women figure so importantly – as mothers, as survivors, as storytellers, as herbalists, as matriarchs, above all as friends – Jewett is implicitly writing against the dominant convention of nineteenth-century fiction, with its emphasis on the sentimental and romantic themes of heterosexual love – courtship, chastity, seduction, marriage. In affirming the importance of the woman-centered world, Jewett, along with other late nineteenth-century local-color writers, was marking an important shift in fictional habits, yet one that did not survive intact into the early twentieth century.[15]

Cather's use of a male narrator implies an acceptance of the more traditional norm of heterosexual narrative, for Jim Burden's fixation is a woman. Yet it is part of the puzzle of *My Ántonia* – as Sharon O'Brien has suggested – that Cather seems to write at times with an emphasis on the difference in gender between Jim and Ántonia, and at times as if gender difference were insignificant, or as if Cather were viewing Ántonia from a female point of view.[16] The inconsistencies in the characterization of the Burden-Ántonia relationship are evident on several key occasions: one notices, for example, the peculiar strength with which Jim says to the Cuzack boys, as he warns them always to be considerate to their mother, "You see I was very much in love with your mother once, and I know there's nobody like her" (390). What is peculiar here is that it seems to endow Jim with a romantic attachment to Ántonia that is seldom otherwise in evidence.

In fact, in a famous passage in "The Hired Girls" section (256–57), Jim offers himself as the subject of a strange conundrum: he has a recurring dream about Lena Lingard, who comes to him in the harvest field and sighs, "Now they are all gone, and I can kiss you as much as I like." Jim wishes he could have this "flattering dream" about Ántonia, but he never does. What's strange is that Jim's "unconscious" will allow him to associate Lena with sexuality, but not Ántonia. What's also strange is that Jim should think this is a "flattering dream," since the image he has of Lena crossing the field toward him is not without a certain menacing aspect: she is carrying, after all, "a curved reaping-hook." Perhaps it's just as well that Jim doesn't imagine Ántonia thus armed.

What are we to make of a passage like this? If Lena is portrayed by Cather as a castrating figure, then Jim doesn't seem to recognize the threat. Is Cather being ironic here, showing us that Jim is not aware of the degree to which his own subconscious is imagining sexuality in threatening terms? Or did Cather include this detail out of some impulse of her own, inadvertently portraying the quasisexual encounter in ambiguous terms?[17]

The scene in which Jim substitutes for Ántonia at Wick Cutter's house (282–83), only to find himself the near-victim of Wick's sexual assault, offers further ambiguities. Though the episode might, in the hands of another author, be treated comically, there is nothing funny about it in Cather's novel, for the aggressive male sexuality of Cutter (note the name) frightens Jim as much as it would frighten any woman. Is the scene telling us that Ántonia was lucky to have escaped a danger to which women are vulnerable? Or that men are equally vulnerable? Interestingly, Wick thinks Ántonia and Jim have been enjoying one another while he is away. But Jim runs away from Wick's house as if it is he who has been raped, and he experiences exorbitant shame at the incident and hatred for Ántonia: "She had let me in for all this disgustingness" (284). And that, we might say, is the closest Jim and Ántonia come to a sexual relationship.

For all his fixation on Ántonia, Jim doesn't in fact experience her as a sexual object. (Cather seems deliberately to have made Jim four years younger than Ántonia; if their ages were reversed, the sexual possibilities might have been stronger.) True, they enjoy some ecstatic moments together in childhood; but these are, we might say, presexual, a kind of prairie Emersonianism (see, e.g., 44–45). Perhaps the closest they both come to ardor is following their hearing of the passionate jazz piano of Blind d'Arnault, whose sensuality is presented in a racial (if not racist) context, as if to draw the line between the African American and Northern European characters: "To hear him, to watch him, was to see a negro enjoying himself as only a negro can. . . . He looked like some glistening African god of pleasure, full of strong, savage blood" (215, 217).[18] Following this excitement, Jim walks Ántonia home, and, as if taking a chill therapy, they stand outside talking "a long while at the Harlings' gate, whispering in the cold until the restlessness was slowly chilled out of us" (219). Later, at the dances, Jim sees Ántonia as "lovely," "with her eyes shining, and her lips always a little parted when she danced"

(254), and he goes so far as to insist on a kiss. (The scene seems as awkward and forced as the kiss itself.) But Ántonia's response to her young friend is always protective rather than sexually engaging, and Jim eventually abandons whatever erotic fantasies he might have and comes to see her primarily in maternal terms: "Her warm, sweet face, her kind arms, and the true heart in her; she was, oh, she was still my Ántonia!" (256) Even more striking is the sentiment Jim expresses at the end of the book, when he says to Ántonia, "I'd have liked to have you for a sweetheart, or a wife, or my mother or my sister – anything that a woman can be to a man" (363). There is a remarkable vagueness in this desire, a willingness to have Ántonia in some "female" way, but without any particular specificity, as if Jim – or Cather – couldn't quite pin down the exact nature of the relationship.

If there is a subtext here, however, it may suggest not so much a lesbian substitution as a regressive fantasy. As Jim feels the "old pull of the earth, the solemn magic that comes out of those fields at nightfall," he wishes, above all, to return to the past: "I wished I could be a little boy again, and that my way could end there" (364). No wonder Jim says, a few pages later, "Some memories are realities, and are better than anything that can ever happen to one again" (370). It is the memory of the past, safely enshrined in those peaceful and protected moments with Ántonia, that most moves Jim, and that seemingly has motivated his narrative in the first place.

As great as the pull of the past is, however, what Cather compels Jim to recognize is the necessity of moving beyond the past into an acceptance of time and change. And here is the most striking difference between Cather and Jewett. When the visitor to Dunnet's Landing in Jewett's volume takes her final leave of the seacoast town, she looks at her empty room and thinks, "I and all my belongings had died out of it." She empathizes with "how it would seem when Mrs. Todd came back and found her lodger gone. So we die before our own eyes; so we see some chapters of our lives come to their natural end" (159). As the boat carrying her back to the city pulls away from the coast, the little town sinks "back into the uniformity of the coast"; and eventually, as the boat continues in its journey, all the coasts "were lost to sight" (160). There is a finality to this leave-taking, a sense that a part of life has died a death both natural and conclusive. That is the serenity in the face of time and change that Jewett offers.

Things are not quite so simple in *My Ántonia*, and here is one major aspect of Cather's revision of Jewett: Jim doesn't leave Black Hawk with a sense of finality, of a closed chapter. He negotiates a relationship to time and change that offers a different kind of serenity from Jewett's.

Jim's earlier return to Ántonia had concluded with his vowing, "I'll come back" (365). Though twenty years pass before his return, he finally fulfills his purpose. In the process, Cather is making some complicated statements about her characters, about memory, and about an engagement with the ongoing stream of life. For it's not enough for Jim simply to rest content with his boyhood memories of Ántonia – that was how Book IV had ended ("The Pioneer Woman's Story"): "As I went back alone over that familiar road, I could almost believe that a boy and girl ran along beside me, as our shadows used to do, laughing and whispering to each other in the grass" (365). When Jim returns in Book V ("Cuzak's Boys") it is as a result of having overcome what had been a persistent obstacle: he had kept putting off a return visit, though he had ample opportunity, because "I did not want to find her aged and broken; I really dreaded it." When he says, a moment later, that "[s]ome memories are realities, and are better than anything that can ever happen to one again" (370), he is speaking, we can see in retrospect, out of a fear that he cannot tolerate the effects of time and change.

But far from endorsing this view, Cather is showing us a quite different view of life; and far from critiquing Jim's romanticism, she is showing us how Jim evolves *beyond* this belief in the pages that follow, depicting the actual encounter with the "aged and broken" Ántonia.

But of course Ántonia is only superficially aged and broken. She stands before him, "a stalwart, brown woman, flat-chested, her curly brown hair a little grizzled" (374). Jim is shocked, but in a moment "the changes grew less apparent to me, her identity stronger. She was there, in the full vigor of her personality, battered but not diminished . . ." (374). She has fewer teeth, but her "inner glow" is intact (379). Jim, by contrast, seems ageless: "You've kept so young, yourself. But it's easier for a man" (378). What makes it even easier, we realize a moment later, is that Jim has not had children. In effect, he has stood outside the stream of generative time, just as Ántonia has chosen to stand squarely inside it: her children press around her, and the farm in general offers a picture of fecund creativity, of swarming life: "Ducks and geese ran quacking across my path. White cats were sunning themselves among yellow pumpkins on the porch steps" (373). The strongest image Jim retains is the moment when Ántonia's children emerge from the sod door of their house: "That moment, when they all came tumbling out of the cave into the light, was a sight any man might have come far to see" (397). Given the Virgilian allusions throughout the novel, it's easy to see Ántonia here in mythic terms, as a creative principle, a source of life's renewal, an earth mother.[19]

In returning to Ántonia, then, Jim is not simply returning to a reality that had otherwise become a series of romanticized images in the memory. He is returning to a reality that is itself taken up with the changing rhythm of seasons, life, growth, birth, and death. If Jim had been previously marginalized in his sterile urban life, here he is at a kind of center of life's renewal. And as he concludes his narrative, it is not only with the sense of "coming home to myself," but with a sense of fusing the future and the past: "Now I understood that the same road was to bring us together again. Whatever we had missed, we possessed together the precious, the incommunicable past" (419). Note the containment of opposites in these two sentences: there is futurity in Jim's conviction that the road will bring them together again, but an opposite confidence in looking back on the past that they "possessed together." (This past is "incommunicable" perhaps in the sense that any strong emotion or image – and Ántonia leaves her mark on Jim through the series of images imprinted on his memory – overwhelms language.)

Yet the ending is paradoxical in yet another sense: for what has Jim done if not communicate with us about the past in the form of his narrative – which was, we recall, itself a "communication" to the editor, placed in her hands at the outset of the book? Cather ends here on an almost Wordsworthian note that leaves us oscillating between Jim's memory of the spots of time in the romantic past, and the affirmation of an ongoing current of time that allows for change, death, renewal, the last of which is achieved, one might say, through the act of writing itself, which is why the *mise en scène* of the narrative – Burden communicating the significance of Ántonia through a manuscript handed to his longtime friend – is so important.

There is one more element in Cather's "revision" of *The Country of the Pointed Firs* that bears examination, and that is the conception of Ántonia herself. In some ways we could liken Ántonia to Mrs. Todd – both are solidly rooted in their communities, both have a closeness to the earth and its mysteries. But we must also say that Ántonia contains, in her history, the possibility of a quite opposite fate, that of Jewett's hermit Joanna, who lives in self-imposed isolation from society. The story of Joanna's exile (told in two segments, "Poor Joanna" and "The Hermitage") is one of the most powerful in *Pointed Firs*, and it forms an interesting counterpoint to the story of Ántonia. Joanna, already dead for twenty years when the story is told, was about to be married when her young man became "bewitched" with another girl. Joanna, who had set her heart on marriage and a home, is devastated, and immediately retires to seclusion on an island owned by her father. There she spends the rest of her days, refusing the pleasures of society, refusing the solace of the Church, living a kind of death-in-life, not thinking herself "fit to live with anybody" (61). She had, in her own eyes, committed the "unpardonable sin": "I was in great wrath and trouble, and my thoughts was so wicked towards God that I can't expect ever to be forgiven" (70). When Mrs. Fosdick, who along with Mrs. Todd is telling this story to the narrator, suggests that nowadays "she'd have gone out West to her uncle's folks or up to Massachusetts and had a change," Mrs. Todd objects. "No," said her friend. " 'T is like bad eyesight, the mind of such a person: if your eyes don't see right there may be a remedy, but there's no kind of glasses to remedy the mind. No, Joanna was Joanna. . . . Some is meant to be the Joannas in this world, an' 't was her poor lot" (72–73).

Ántonia, like Joanna, is disappointed in her first love. Her plans to marry the boastful conductor Larry Donovan come to ruin when Donovan deserts the pregnant Ántonia, and she must return in shame to Black Hawk. But rather than lead a life of self-imposed guilt or exile, Ántonia rebounds: she marries a fellow Bohemian immigrant, Cuzak, and the two beget a family bursting with energy and good humor. The romantic Larry Donovan yields to the more prosaic Cuzak; but Ántonia and her husband are devoted to one another, as devoted as good friends, and their relationship becomes the foundation for Ántonia's renewed life, rooted in family, earth, and the cycles of the farm seasons. Ántonia, we might say, suffered the experience of a Joanna but became, despite it all, a Mrs. Todd. (We recall Cather's negative review of Kate Chopin's *The Awakening* in 1899, which criticized Chopin's overemphasis on romantic love and found the disappointed heroine's suicide an illustration of "unbalanced idealism.")[20] Cather was also, of course, revising Hester Prynne's story, showing us a "ruined" woman allowed to lead a socially approved, fulfilled life without having to sublimate her revolutionary impulses into a socially acceptable penitential role, as did the Puritan woman.

Jewett's story of Joanna had been set in the past – i.e., the post–Civil War period – and it illustrates for Jewett a shift in the master plots that governed cultural values, from the mentality of a Joanna to the mentality of a Mrs. Todd. While Joanna is ruled by the stories of courtship and marriage, whose obverse is the story of tragic disappointment and suicide, Mrs. Todd is governed by stories of survival, of the values of community and of female friendship that transcend romantic love. Jewett was framing the older tragic love narrative by a newer narrative; and in this she is, we might say, juxtaposing an older narrative story with a newer one, offering us a critique of the older one and at the same time presenting it as a living memory within the community of women's storytelling.

Cather, too, is "writing beyond the ending" of traditional nineteenth-century fiction, to borrow Rachel DuPlessis' term, though in a different way.[21] Her story of Ántonia offers a comic resolution (in the Shakespearian sense) to the potentially tragic fate that seemed to lie in wait for the ruined immigrant girl. Ántonia has, we know, her moment of misery. But she comes through it to an optimistic mastery of life's forces that Cather celebrates. Moreover, as the book concludes, we experience a deepened contrast between the two characters: Jim Burden's great worldly power ("legal counsel for one of the great Western railways") seems to pale beside the greater spiritual and natural power of Ántonia, with her impressive progeny.[22] Yet Jim has achieved by the book's conclusion a kind of serenity of his own: he has recognized the great power of nature – "time and change" – not only to renew but to obliterate our human efforts (the old road out to Black Hawk, he sees, has been partly ploughed under and partly erased by the forces of nature), and he has come to terms with it all.

But if we step back from the text and look again at its relation to Jewett and to *The Country of the Pointed Firs*, we find some puzzling questions. If we can say Cather "revised" Jewett, it was in the direction of what is in some ways a softer, more optimistic vision of life. True, there is Mr. Shimerda's suicide and Pavel's story of the bride thrown to the wolves; but these episodes seem, by the end of the book, part of a distant place or a distant time, almost a part of legend. The tragic fate of a Joanna is not of interest to Cather, nor are the other lives of hermetic isolation, stifled expression, and loss that Jewett writes about in *Pointed Firs*. And, as I have been arguing, the finality of the narrator's departure in Jewett is softened, in Cather, into a deepening of the ties between Jim and Ántonia's family that will go beyond the ending of the book itself (at least Jim is confident of their continuing bond). If we accept this view of the relationship between the two books, then Cather seems to be fulfilling her mentor's advice to write books that would be spiritually encouraging and to avoid the "danger" of pessimism. In a letter to one of Cather's *McClure's* colleagues who had sent her Cather's early collection of stories, *The Troll Garden*, Jewett wrote, displaying a surprising impatience for the kind of story she herself told so well:

I cannot help wishing that a writer of such promise chose rather to show the hopeful, *constructive* yes – even the pleasant side of unpleasant things and disappointed lives! Is not this what we are bound to do in our own lives and still more bound to do as writers? I shrink more and more from anything that looks like giving up the game.

As Sharon O'Brien suggests in examining this passage, we can assume Cather was shown Jewett's letter.[23] We cannot be entirely sure how much weight to give to Jewett's influence here, but certainly the dedication of the optimistic *O Pioneers!* to Jewett's memory (she had died a few years before) is consistent with this reading of the relationship.

What is puzzling, however, is how Cather characterizes Jewett's work when she talks about it after Jewett's death. In the 1925 Preface to Jewett's fiction, for example, she describes the triumph of Jewett's fiction within terms that seem almost too small: the stories "have much to do with fisher-folk and seaside villages; with juniper pastures and lonely farms, neat gray country houses and delightful, well-seasoned old men and women. . . . There may be Othellos and Iagos and Don Juans, but they are not highly characteristic of the country, they do not come up spontaneously in the juniper pastures as the everlasting does. Miss Jewett wrote of the people who grew out of the soil and the life of the country near her heart, not about exceptional individuals at war with their environment." And she recalls Jewett saying that "her head was full of dear old houses and dear old women, and that when an old house and an old woman came together in her brain with a click, she knew that a story was under way" (Preface, 9). Cather may be trying to distance Jewett from an outmoded naturalism here (as indeed Jewett herself had come to feel that naturalism's extremes and pessimism were outmoded), but as a representation of the stories in *The Country of the Pointed Firs*, this preface is seriously misleading. The stories of *Pointed Firs* – though they surely do have the quality of the ordinary Cather is highlighting here – also have a quite different quality. Many of Jewett's most notable characters (not Mrs. Todd, to be sure) are grotesques whose lives have been distorted by their experience, who *are* in some ways "exceptional individuals at war with their environment." Indeed, it is precisely the tension between the ordinary and the extraordinary that is most characteristic of Jewett's art at its finest.

It is as if Cather – in the Preface to *Pointed Firs*, and in *My Ántonia* considered as a "revision" of the former book – is suppressing one side of Jewett's art, the narrations of tragic isolation and despondency, in favor of a sweeter, more optimistic side. One can only speculate as to why Cather should have thus "revised" Jewett. If we follow Harold Bloom into the labyrinths of poetic influence, with all its contradictions, we might say that an essential aspect of Cather's self-definition was a "misreading" of Jewett, yet one that conformed in a way to Jewett's own advice to her to shun the darkly pessimistic.[24] Or possibly it was a "misreading" prompted by denial: on another level we can see Cather's optimism in the face of time and change as a reaction (we might even call it a healthy reaction) to Cather's own deeply felt loss of her companion and friend Isabelle McClung, who had married the year Cather began writing *My Ántonia*. In this context, the novel becomes a way of allowing Jim to live constructively with his own sense of loss, and to say, in effect, *there is no loss*, you can go home again.

This essay has been, for the most part, a retrospective reading of Cather, exploring the significance and the ambiguities of her relationship with Jewett. But what seems finally important to add, as a last perspective, is the place Cather occupies within the generation of American writers beginning to establish themselves in the first decades of the twentieth century. For in establishing a nineteenth-century lineage for Jewett (and for herself) in the issue of time and change, Cather was asserting not so much a nineteenth-century concern as a concern of the early twentieth century. It is as an aspect of Cather's modernism, finally, that we may see *My Ántonia*, a work that anticipates the concern with time that will emerge as a central issue in the work of Fitzgerald, Hemingway, and Faulkner.[25] For Cather, as for these others, the struggle to define a structure of value in a world that assailed the writer with images of banality, commercialism, greed, squalor, and violence, led to a privileging of the past in a form that was often more than tinged with romanticism. If Cather anticipated a major preoccupation of modernist writing – the discovery of a balance between the past and the future, a positioning of the subject within time and change in a way that denied neither the past nor the evolving future – her distinction was likewise to have arrived at serenity not through any dodge of escapism but rather through the complex representation of a deeply personal engagement with the problem of change.

NOTES

1. Willa Cather, "Preface" (1925), *The Country of the Pointed Firs and Other Stories*, by Sarah Orne Jewett (Garden City: Doubleday, 1956), p. 11. Future references to the Preface are incorporated into the text.

2. Willa Cather, *My Ántonia* (New York: Houghton Mifflin, 1918 and 1926), p. ix. Future references will be incorporated into the text in parentheses.

3. Willa Cather, *My Ántonia*, in *Willa Cather: Early Novels and Stories*, Library of America series, edited by Sharon O'Brien (New York: Literary Classics of the United States), p. 714.

4. Nathaniel Hawthorne, *The Scarlet Letter*, Norton Critical Edition, second edition (New York: W. W. Norton, 1978), p. 29.

5. Ferris Greenslet, *Under the Bridge* (Boston: Houghton, 1943), p. 119. Quoted in James Woodress, "The Making and Reception of *My Ántonia*," in Susan J. Rosowski, ed., *Approaches to Teaching Cather's My Ántonia* (New York: Modern Language Association, 1989), p. 40.

6. Willa Cather, "Sarah Orne Jewett," *Not Under Forty* (New York: Knopf, 1936), p. 93.

7. Written 1928, "Neighbour Rosicky" deals with a family similar to the one Ántonia and Cuzack have established by the end of *My Ántonia*, and it evinces antiurban sentiment even more obviously: Rosicky has lived in cities but chooses deliberately to escape from them to the Midwest and land ownership. On the farm, "You didn't have to choose between bosses and strikers, and go wrong either way. You didn't have to do with dishonest and cruel people.

... In the country, if you had a mean neighbour, you could keep off his land and make him keep off yours. But in the city, all the foulness and misery and brutality of your neighbours was part of your life.'' *Obscure Destinies* (New York: Alfred Knopf, 1941), p. 59.

8. See Sharon O'Brien, *Willa Cather: The Emerging Voice* (New York: Oxford, 1987), especially chapters 15 and 16.

9. Willa Cather, *The Kingdom of Art: Willa Cather's First Principles and Critical Statements, 1893–1896*, edited by Bernice Slote (Lincoln: University of Nebraska Press,1966), p. 449.

10. For an excellent discussion of the friendship between Cather and Jewett and of the creative psychology underlying Cather's debt to the older writer, see O'Brien, *Willa Cather*, esp. pp. 334–363.

11. Cf. Jewett's description of Mrs. Todd: ''She might belong to any age, like an idyl of Theocritus.'' *Country of the Pointed Firs*, p. 56.

12. Willa Cather, ''The Novel Demeublée,'' in *On Writing: Critical Studies on Writing as an Art* (New York: Knopf, 1949), pp. 35–43.

13. See Miles Orvell, *The Real Thing: Imitation and Authenticity in American Culture, 1880–1940* (Chapel Hill: University of North Carolina Press, 1989), pp. 141–156.

14. See especially, in *The Professor's House*, the characterization of Tom Outland's journal, which the professor is annotating, and in which the minute descriptions of objects, tools, pottery, have a moral as well as an aesthetic quality: ''To St. Peter this plain account was almost beautiful, because of the stupidities it avoided and the things it did not say. . . . The adjectives were purely descriptive, relating to form and colour, and were used to present the objects under consideration, not the young explorer's emotions'' (New York: Knopf, 1925; p. 262). In passages like this – which echo Cather's critical statements – the writer sounds almost like Ezra Pound offering his list of rules for writing the new poetry.

15. See Josephine Donovan, *New England Local Color Literature: A Women's Tradition* (New York: Ungar, 1983).

16. See Sharon O'Brien, ''Gender, Sexuality, and Point of View: Teaching *My Ántonia* from a Feminist Perspective,'' in Susan J. Rosowski, ed., *Approaches to Teaching Cather's My Ántonia* (New York: Modern Language Association, 1989), pp. 140–45.

17. See Blanche Gelfant's more general discussion of sexuality in *My Ántonia*, ''The Forgotten Reaping-Hook: Sex in *My Ántonia*,'' *American Literature* 43 (1971): 60–82; reprinted in John J. Murphy, ed., *Critical Essays on Willa Cather* (Boston: G. K. Hall, 1984).

18. Cf. Eudora Welty's characterization of the African American jazz piano player in her story "Powerhouse."

19. There is a Keatsian echo to Cather's conception as well, and also a revision of Keats. Elizabeth Sergeant records the moment in her memoirs when, in 1916, as she was about to write *My Ántonia*, Cather spoke fervently about her heroine while placing on the table an "old Sicilian apothecary jar": "I want my new heroine to be like this – like a rare object in the middle of a table, which one may examine from all sides." [Elizabeth Sergeant, *Willa Cather: A Memoir* (Lincoln: University of Nebraska Press, 1963), p. 139.] One thinks, inevitably, of Keats's Grecian urn, which the poet likewise examined from all sides and which similarly evoked a set of imagined scenes. But there is this difference between Cather's apothecary jar and Keats's urn, which makes *My Ántonia* at bottom a refutation of Keats. Keats, looking at the frozen pictures on the Grecian urn, celebrates their undying life, their removal from the stream of time and change and suffering and sees in the permanence of their aesthetic distance a saving function for humankind:
When old age shall this generation waste,
Thou shalt remain, in midst of other woe
Than ours, a friend to man, to whom thou say'st,
Beauty is truth, truth beauty, – that is all,
Ye know on earth, and all ye need to know.
Cather, exploring the process of remembering Ántonia, sets her not at a safe remove from life, but precisely in the stream of time and change, and requires Jim to come to terms with her as an aspect of human mortality. The source of "serenity" in Keats is an aesthetic refuge; in Cather, it is mortal growth and change.

20. Cather wrote, "These people really expect the passion of love to fill and gratify every need of life, whereas nature only intended that it should meet one of many demands." "Books and Magazines," Pittsburgh *Leader* (July 8, 1899), p. 6. Reprinted in *The Awakening*, by Kate Chopin, edited by Margaret Culley, Norton Critical Edition (New York: W. W. Norton, 1976), p. 153–55.

21. See Rachel Blau DuPlessis, *Writing beyond the Ending: Narrative Strategies of Twentieth-Century Women Writers* (Bloomington: Indiana University Press, 1985).

22. In some ways, the symbiotic tension that Cather establishes between Jim and Ántonia by the end of the book echoes one of the most memorable images in *My Ántonia* – the image of the plough against the horizon. As Jim, Ántonia, and Lena watch the sun set, they discern what appears to be a "great black figure" against the

setting sun. They realize, in a moment, that it is a plough that has
been left in a field, but the image of the thing, "contained within
the circle of the disc . . . black against the molten red" is awe-
inspiring. "There it was, heroic in size, a picture writing on the
sun" (278–279). Whether or not we choose to think of the swords
of the explorers (Jim has just been talking about the Spanish con-
querers) being beaten into the farmer's ploughshares, we have in
this image an emblem of domination, of conquest of the land, of
taking control technologically of raw nature. As such, we may associate it with Jim, who extends that form of conquest into the
development of the railway lines. But the chapter ends on a final
paragraph that places this image within a different context, though
it has seldom been noted. For as the "ball" of the sun drops down
and the fields grow dark, Jim writes that the "forgotten plough
had sunk back to its own littleness somewhere on the prairie"
(279). In other words, we conclude with an image of nature finally
overpowering the puny force of human effort, and it suggests a
respect for the power of nature, over and beyond our efforts to
"conquer" the land. And as such, it is an adumbration of Ántonia,
or of how we will come to see her by the end of the narrative,
identified with the life forces of nature, accepting her limitations,
content with the finite ambitions of her life.

23. Sarah Orne Jewett to Witter Bynner, May 3, 1905, Houghton Library, Harvard University, Cambridge, Mass. Quoted in O'Brien,
Willa Cather, p. 343.

24. "We know, as Blake did, that Poetic Influence is gain and loss,
inseparably wound in the labyrinth of history." Bloom argues that
we must read "any poem as its poet's deliberate misinterpretation,
as a poet, of a precursor poem." Harold Bloom, *The Anxiety of Influence: A Theory of Poetry* (New York: Oxford, 1966), pp. 29, 43.

25. Cf. the very Catheresque sentiment (if not sentence) that ends *The
Great Gatsby*: "So we beat on, boats against the current, borne back
ceaselessly into the past."

3

My Ántonia and
African American Art

ELIZABETH AMMONS

> When Dvorak wrote his "American Symphony,"
> did he or did he not in certain parts copy
> the music of the American Negro? This is
> the question. It is not denied that he was
> influenced by Negro melodies, but how far?
>   – The Crisis (1911)[1]

JIM Burden says of Blind d'Arnault in *My Ántonia* (1918) that he had "the soft, amiable Negro voice, like those I remembered from early childhood, with the note of docile subservience in it. He had the Negro head, too; almost no head at all; nothing behind the ears but folds of neck under close-clipped wool."[2] His mother, we learn, was "a buxom young Negro wench" (185); he himself as a child was a "hideous little pickaninny" (186). As an adult he is the embodiment of spontaneity and abandon: "To hear him, to watch him, was to see a Negro enjoying himself as only a Negro can" (189). Seated at the piano, "he looked like some glistening African god of pleasure, full of strong savage blood" (191).

It is not surprising that little criticism exists about Blind d'Arnault.[3] His presentation contains so many stereotypes that most discussions of Cather have shrunk from considering him. Yet precisely because the characterization is offensive, Blind d'Arnault demands attention. Denying Cather's racism will not make it go away.

A second reason for thinking about Blind d'Arnault is that he is crucial to the novel. If the black piano player is insulted, he also is presented as a musical genius – the highest possible praise from Cather, for whom music represented the supreme art

57

form.[4] As a small child living on an antebellum plantation, d'Arnault could not resist music. Despite threats of punishment, the boy had to get to the piano in the Big House:

Through the dark he found his way to the Thing, to its mouth. He touched it softly, and it answered softly, kindly. He shivered and stood still. Then he began to feel it all over, ran his finger-tips along the slippery sides, embraced the carved legs, tried to get some conception of its shape and size, of the space it occupied in primeval night. It was cold and hard, and like nothing else in his black universe. He went back to its mouth, began at one end of the keyboard and felt his way down into the mellow thunder, as far as he could go. He seemed to know that it must be done with the fingers, not with the fists or the feet. He approached this highly artificial instrument through a mere instinct, and coupled himself to it, as if he knew it was to piece him out and make a whole creature of him. (187–88)

This relationship to music is immediate, total, obsessive. D'Arnault embodies the driving passion – indeed, compulsion – often associated with the high artist in the modern West. He needs music even as other people need food and water: "He wore his teachers out. He could never learn like other people, never acquired any finish. He was always a Negro prodigy who played barbarously and wonderfully. As piano-playing, it was perhaps abominable, but as music it was something real, vitalized by a sense of rhythm that was stronger than his other physical senses – that not only filled his dark mind, but worried his body incessantly" (189). The racism here is obvious – the adverb "barbarously," the term "creature," the emphasis on "rhythm" and darkness. Yet these descriptions also single out d'Arnault, like Ántonia's father, Mr. Shimerda, as the born artist.

It is significant that the two premier artists in Cather's novel about a repressed well-educated white man's attempt to make art – to express the story of Ántonia in some way that might do justice to who she is – are not elite university-trained men, but instead an impoverished eastern European immigrant and a blind African American.[5] Each takes an elite European instrument – the violin, the piano – and creates powerful vernacular art. They fuse classical and peasant traditions to generate vibrant "folk" music, which, we can infer, Jim Burden must also do if he truly wishes to find an adequate way to tell Ántonia's story. His struggle to render Ántonia produces one of the book's major fascinations, the text's shifting, complicated gap between narrator and narrated subject.[6]

But my interest here is in d'Arnault. Why a black musician? And why does he erupt out of nowhere late in Cather's novel set in America's heartland? My discussion approaches d'Arnault both as a character and as a signifier of repressed African American art in *My Ántonia*. I argue that Cather simultaneously celebrates and demeans the pianist because her novel is deeply indebted to and shaped by African American music, yet she was conflicted about that debt. Therefore she signals the influence that black music had on her (Blind d'Arnault's presence in the text) but at the same time denies and disowns it (the racist undercutting). To explore this contradiction, I consider four related topics that bear on *My Ántonia*: Cather's attitudes about race and her racism; African American music at the turn of the century; the real-life black pianists upon whom Cather modeled d'Arnault; and Toni Morrison's paradigmatic critical concept of the "ghost in the machine."

* * * * *

Although Willa Cather is most commonly thought of in connection with the Great Plains and the Southwest, she was born and raised in the South. She spent the first nine years of her life in Virginia, where, as she explicitly states at the end of her last published novel, *Sapphira and the Slave Girl* (1940), the lives and stories of African Americans affected her indelibly.

This last novel tells the story of a jealous white woman, Sapphira Colbert, who plots the rape of her young black slave Nancy Till, who escapes through the aid of Sapphira's grown daughter, Rachel Blake – a woman Cather based on her own maternal grandmother, Rachel Boak.[7] What matters most to my discussion is the fact that Cather includes herself in the novel for the only time in her career. She writes herself into the Epilogue as a five-year-old to make the point that Nancy's story, which she identifies as the most important in the book, was part of her – Willa Cather's – real past. The Epilogue states:

Ever since I could remember anything, I had heard about Nancy. My mother used to sing me to sleep with:
Down by de cane-brake, close by de mill,
Dar lived a yaller gal, her name was Nancy Till.
I never doubted the song was made about our Nancy.[8]

Cather admits here that her earliest memory ("ever since I could remember anything") was music from and about African American life. As she learned to invent her own patterns of language and narrative, the music that rocked her to sleep came out of, or was inspired by, African American culture.

As Sharon O'Brien explains, Willa Cather often emphasized the importance to her of Nancy Till's story: "The 'Epilogue' to *Sapphira* was literally true, every word of it, Cather insisted to friends, and it described the greatest event of her Virginia years: when Nancy Till, the slave girl who had fled to Canada before the Civil War, returned to Willow Shade to be reunited with her aging mother."[9] Willa Cather knew that her early exposure to African American people and culture had profoundly affected her.

Yet what she did with that influence, even in *Sapphira*, the book in which she acknowledged her debt, presents major problems. The novel is full of racist stereotypes. The narrator refers to "the emotional darkies" (70); the fat black cook rolls her eyes "like black-and-white china marbles" (100); Nancy displays "the foolish, dreamy, nigger side of her nature" (178); and the head millhand Sampson, very much like d'Arnault, is described in subhuman terms: "His head was full behind the ears, shaped more like a melon lying down than a peanut standing on end" (109). Even worse, the slaves Cather imagines are totally passive. Although some white characters in *Sapphira* hate slavery, no black people even question the institution. Nancy attempts her escape only because Rachel, a white woman, virtually forces her to. Most disturbing, however, is Cather's appropriation of Nancy's story to tell her own. The black woman does not exist as the agent of her own drama but as the pretext for Cather's telling the *real* story of *Sapphira and the Slave Girl*: her own genesis as an artist out of a long line of strong-minded white women.[10]

While most obvious perhaps in *Sapphira*, Cather's racism is hardly limited to one or two texts. Throughout her career, she accepted white supremacist race theories which characterized dark-skinned and Semitic people – African Americans, Asians and Asian Americans, Mexicans and Mexican Americans, Native Americans, Jews – as inferior to whites. As Cather criticism has reluctantly begun to recognize (much more work remains to be done), Willa Cather was not somehow above and untouched by her environment. She readily participated in mainstream racist attitudes prevalent early in the twentieth century.[11]

How are we to read this racism today? Is it legitimate for us, almost a century later, to judge the attitudes of an author who lived and wrote ninety years ago? The clear answer is yes. Cather's racist stereotypes and ethnocentric biases were no less reductive, distorting, and insulting in the early twentieth century than in the late twentieth century. Consider W. E. B. Du Bois' angry criticism in 1913 that "everything touching the Negro is banned by magazines and publishers unless it takes the form of caricature or bitter attack, or is so thoroughly innocuous as to have no literary flavor."[12] Equally emphatic is the sarcastic inversion of stereotypes expressed in *Mrs. Spring Fragrance* (1912) by Sui Sin Far, a woman of Asian heritage who published fiction in the United States about Chinese American experience: "Many American women wrote books. Why should not a Chinese? She would write a book about Americans for her Chinese women friends. The American people were so *interesting* and *mysterious*."[13] Or there is the outrage about Cather's *Death Comes for the Archbishop* (1927) voiced by Mary Austin, Cather's contemporary and a middle-aged white woman like herself: "Miss Cather used my house to write in, but she did not tell me what she was doing. When it was finished, I was very much distressed to find that she had given her allegiance to the French blood of the Archbishop; she had sympathized with his desire to build a French cathedral in a Spanish town. It was a calamity to the local culture. We have never got over it."[14] Objecting to racism and ethnocentricity in American literature is not a late twentieth-century invention, a superimposition of historically illegitimate notions onto the past. Cather's attitudes toward people of color and minority cultures in the United States, even if typical of mainstream, dominant-culture attitudes of her day, were objectionable then as well as now. In particular, rationalizing Cather's failure to rise above bigoted racial attitudes at the same time that we praise her for enlightened attitudes toward certain European immigrants or certain groups of women represents the height of willful delusion. Willa Cather shared and acted upon standard white racist attitudes of her day, and that fact must be stated and faced. Her attitudes have always been offensive and injurious, as people such as W. E. B. Du Bois, Sui Sin Far, and Mary Austin have declared.

At the same time – and this is what makes Blind d'Arnault's presence in *My Ántonia* complex – as an artist, Cather was drawn to black culture. As her Epilogue to *Sapphira* admits, her earliest musical and narrative impressions came from African American life. That strong influence and debt were especially hard to suppress – keep under control – in *My Ántonia*, a book conceived at a time when black music, in the form of ragtime, constituted the creatively most important, distinctly "American" music.

* * * * *

For African Americans the turn of the century, in the words of the historian Rayford W. Logan, was "the nadir."[15] Racism had dismantled Reconstruction, creating a situation of neo-slavery for many southern black Americans. At the same time, throughout the nation, Jim Crow laws institutionalized segregation, economic discrimination ran rampant, and the incidence of lynching increased. To support and rationalize this intensifying racism, a prolific, reactionary literature burgeoned. Articles, books, pamphlets, tracts, sermons, novels, and speeches attacked the intelligence, the industriousness, the morality, and even the biological evolution of black people. The strategy was simple: If white people could "prove" the inferiority of people of color, then economic exploitation and institutionalized violence, from rape to lynching, could, at least for many white Americans, be justified.

For example, in 1918, the year that *My Ántonia* was published, Americans could buy *The Truth About Lynching and the Negro in the South, In Which the Author Pleads That the South Be Made Safe for the White Race*, by Winfield H. Collins, M.A., Ph.D. Collins maintains that the black man "with all his barbarism and ignorance [is] totally unrelated to the white man in origin, character, and race" and describes "the Negro" as "son of a wild and tropical race, content for thousands of years to roam the jungles of Africa, supplied by bountiful nature with all his heart's desire, failing thus to develop any controlling trait of character, or mental stamina."[16] The book asserts that "the Negro is woefully lacking in initiative and persistence" and contends that African Americans (along with Filipinos, whom Collins also says "are not fit for self-government") "would be greatly benefited by some sort of probationary oversight" (98). To support this thesis Collins argues that "a great part of them are no more fit to profit by their freedom than so many children" (98). Probably most vehement is Collins' attack on black leaders who have the audacity to demand that lynching be made a federal crime: "Such talk as this serves to promote Negro crime" (100).

Views such as Collins' had such wide currency among whites in turn-of-the-century America that a vigorous counterliterature was produced by African Americans and by a few sympathetic whites in order to fight back.[17] Also, direct political response, as Collins' reference to African American leaders suggests, grew in strength. In 1909, for instance, the National Association for the Advancement of Colored People, the nation's oldest civil rights organization, was formed.

In this climate of racist attack and increasing resistance in the black community, African American art flourished. In literature, the 1890s and the first two decades of the twentieth century saw the production of major work by Frances Ellen Harper, Charles Chesnutt, Paul Laurence Dunbar, Pauline Hopkins, W. E. B. Du Bois, James Weldon Johnson, Alice Dunbar-Nelson, and Jessie Redmon Fauset. New black periodicals such as *The Colored American Magazine* (1900–1909), under the editorial leadership of Pauline Hopkins during its first four years, and *The Crisis*, founded in

1910 as the official publication of the NAACP, emerged. They published large quantities of creative work and also ran numerous stories about African American artists working in all media – painting, sculpture, drama, fiction, poetry, and, of most interest to this discussion, music.

Most striking in the discussions of music in these two turn-of-the-century black periodicals is their impatience with white America's exclusive interest in ragtime. In 1902 the famous black opera performer and manager Theodore Drury opens "The Negro in Classic Music; Or, Leading Opera, Oratorio and Concert Singers," an article in the *Colored American*, with: "It has generally been supposed that the Negro could not, and moreover would never be able to, sing classic music; presumably for the reason those heard most often nearly always sing rag-time music. There are, however, singers among the race who are devoting their best efforts to a higher class of music, and to these I shall devote my time and space."[18] Featuring Drury in an article about opera earlier that same year, Robert W. Carter similarly contends that, despite the fact that "the white race thinks the Negro is at home in no place in the theatrical world but on the comic stage," black Americans have distinguished themselves in all types of music, including classical.[19] The next year Carter, who had emphasized in his 1902 essay that he had nothing against ragtime but, rather, against white assumptions that black people could create and perform nothing but ragtime, again focused on Drury in the *Colored American*.[20] Writing in 1904 about the singer Hamilton Hodges and his celebrated performance of works by the black composer Samuel Coleridge-Taylor, Pauline Hopkins also stresses the diversity of black music. After summarizing the Fisk Jubilee Singers' accomplishments, she points out: "From that period until the present time, the Negro has developed rapidly along musical lines, easily floating into the best society and accumulating a competency in foreign countries by his musical gifts.[21]

Profiles of musicians in the *Crisis* a decade later echo the *Colored American*'s interest in countering stereotypes. The *Crisis*'s "Men of the Month" section routinely included musicians, featuring in 1912, for example, a profile of the composer (and brother of James Weldon Johnson) J. Rosamond Johnson, who is called "the most versatile composer of colored America and one of the striking musical geniuses of the land" (March 1912: 190). Of the composer Samuel Coleridge-Taylor, who is compared to Grieg and Brahms because they drew on European folk traditions, the writer says: "Mr. Coleridge-Taylor, intensely racial, found his deepest inspiration in the Negro folk song" (Oct. 1912: 278). Likewise, of Will Marion Cook it is said that his "present serious work is the development of Negro folklore in dance forms for chamber music. He feels that the Negro in music will have to take his place through the development of the old melodies, the songs of the slaves and old religious croonings" (Dec. 1912: 67).

Underlying the black press's desire to call attention to the diversity of black music and to the incorporation of traditional vernacular forms into serious new (elite) art was the fact that ragtime remained the rage. The *Crisis* quotes the Los Angeles *Times* in 1913: "It may be news to some, but the wave of ragtime at present sweeping America (also, by the way, washing out considerable starch from the British composition) is really a triumph for the colored race." The *Times* article says ragtime is eighteen years old and attributes its origin to "Will Cook, a splendid musician, as so many Negroes are. Cook started it with a libretto by Paul Dunbar, whose face was as black as his lines were brilliant." The essay marvels: "Only eighteen years ago; and this African renaissance has captured the human race!" The article points to ragtime echoes not only in Dvorak but also in Cather's favorite composer, Wagner, saying "the extollers of Wagner are in reality praising ragtime raised to a dramatic height." Perhaps most interesting to a consideration of artistic creation in the United States in the early twentieth century is the article's contention that rag as a form has saturated American life. People "are beginning to think and talk and act in ragtime." Everything is being syncopated, even conversation and political speeches" (April 1913: 276).

As music historian James Lincoln Collier explains, syncopation in ragtime is actually a misnomer. Ragtime "is essentially a piano music. Its roots lie in the attempt by American blacks of the eighteenth and nineteenth centuries to replicate in their music something of the cross-rhythms that were at the heart of African music." Collier points out:

In their efforts to understand this and similar figures in their own terms, whites, and blacks educated in the European musical system, saw as syncopation this "ragging" of the melody, as it came to be called. The term "syncopation" is applied to a note or figure that begins between the beats or is arranged so that its principal notes fall between the beats. . . . The reader can get something of the feel of syncopation by clapping his hands between his footfalls as he walks.

But syncopation is a European device, not an African one. What looked like syncopation to white transcribers were actually cross-rhythms. The notes were not being set precisely between the beats, but were placed slightly ahead of the beat or behind it. Phrases were stretched out of their natural length; notes were jumped in early. The general effect was a lifting away of the melody from the time scheme, detaching it from the beat so that it seemed to float above it.[22]

Although the connection is not typically made, ragtime, with its exploitation of folk materials and its cross-rhythmic manipulation of space and structure, bears consideration as one major source of inspiration for modernist form in art. Specifically, it seems to me that rag-inspired form can be read as one buried but nevertheless important organizing principle in *My Ántonia* – in which, to borrow Collier's language and apply it to Cather's narrative, we can think of "phrases"/scenes being "stretched out of their natural length" or of the "lifting away of the melody [Ántonia's story] from the time scheme" (Jim's life) to create the effect of narrative "floating" above time. Cather hints (in spite of herself) at this African American musical presence in the surprising, abrupt appearance in the novel of her fictitious popular black pianist, d'Arnault.

* * * * *

Historically, there were two obvious real-life models for Blind d'Arnault: the well-known midwestern traveling pianist and ragger Blind Boone and, preceding Boone, the famous slave child-prodigy and then adult pianist, Blind Tom. Although biographers mention that Cather attended performances by both men,[23] detailed discussion of them and of black music in *My Ántonia* does not exist.

Blind Tom was enormously popular in the second half of the nineteenth century. He performed from New York to California, toured Europe, and played at the White House, amazing audiences with his original compositions, his renditions of thousands of well known compositions and, above all, his ability to hear once and then flawlessly play back any music. James M. Trotter offers an excellent description in his opening paragraph about Tom in *Music and Some Highly Musical People* (1881):

He is unquestionably and conspicuously the most wonderful musician the world has ever known. No one has ever equalled him in quickness and depth of musical insight and feeling, nor in the constancy with which he bears within himself, in all its fulness, that mysterious power which can be called by no truer name than *musical inspiration*. . . . We often speak of those who have an "ear for music." Here is a musician who surpasses all others in all the world in the possession of this quality; for his is a *perfect ear*. You may sit down to the piano-forte, and strike any note or chord or discord, or a great number of them; and he will at once give their proper names, and, taking your place, reproduce them. Complete master of the piano-forte keyboard, he calls to his melodious uses, with most consummate ease, all of its resources that are known to skilful performers, as well as constantly discovers and applies those that are new. Under his magnetic touch, this instrument may become, at his will, a *music-box*, a *hand-organ*, a *harp* or a *bagpipe*, a "*Scotch fiddle*," a *church-organ*, a *guitar*, or a *banjo*: it may imitate the "stump speaker" as he delivers his glowing harangue; or, being brought back to its legitimate tones, it may be made to sing two melodies at once, while the performer with his voice delivers a third, all three in different time and keys, all in perfect tune and time, and each one easily distinguishable from the other! It would be vain to call such performances as these mere tricks. They are far, far more; since they show a musical intuition, and an orderly disposition and marshalling of the stores of the mind, quite beyond the powers of the performer of mere musical tricks.

Trotter quotes an anonymous fan's declaration: " 'There is music in all things; but "Blind Tom" is the temple wherein music dwells.' "[24]

Born Thomas Greene Bethune near Columbus, Georgia, on May 25, 1849, Blind Tom was the son of slave parents bought in 1850 by a Columbus lawyer named Colonel Bethune. He seems to have been in some way mentally handicapped, perhaps what would be called an *idiot savant* today. As Tom's modern biographer Geneva H. Southall explains, Bethune ruthlessly exploited the musical prodigy. Before the Civil War, all of Tom's earnings were taken by Bethune or other whites to whom Bethune hired him out – and those earnings were considerable. For example, in one three-year period, Tom brought in more than $50,000.[25] Supposedly free after the war, Tom remained enslaved by Bethune, who wrote a contract giving himself 90 percent and Tom 10 percent of his income. This exploitation continued as successive white guardian-managers took over from the Colonel. As Southall points out, the amount of money stolen from Blind Tom was enormous: "Black historian Edward Scobie has discovered that Tom's 1866 London concerts brought over $100,000 to his managers."[26]

Exploited economically, Tom was also sensationalized to support racist stereotypes. Billed and then described in the white press as an idiot, he was also said by his managers to be totally without musical instruction. In fact, he did receive some training, both from members of the Bethune family and from professional musicians.[27] Geneva Southall suggests that Tom was said to be untrained in order to heighten audiences' amazement. In addition and even more pernicious, as Southall points out, his white managers probably encouraged his bizarre behavior on stage – no matter what his ordinary mental capacity might have been – so that white stereotypes of the inarticulate, animalistic, black man would be fulfilled.[28]

Typical of the way Blind Tom was perceived by whites is Rebecca Harding Davis' description in the 1862 *Atlantic Monthly*. In contrast to the way the African American writer Trotter, quoted above, describes Tom, Davis imagines him as a "picaninny." She visualizes "but a lump of black flesh, born blind, and with the vacant grin of idiocy, they thought, already stamped on his face." She pictures him on the kitchen floor "stupid, flabby, sleepy," and then declares: "The boy, creeping about day after day in the hot light, was as repugnant an object as the lizards in the neighboring swamps." She theorizes that "he was of the lowest negro type, from which only field-hands can be made, – coal-black, with protruding heels, the ape-jaw, blubber-lips constantly open, the sightless eyes closed, and the head thrown far back on the shoulders, lying on the back, in fact, a habit which he still retains, and which adds to the imbecile character of the face." Davis shows us Tom at a concert reluctantly seating "himself at last before the piano, a full half-yard distant, stretching out his arms full-length, like an ape clawing for food." Contradicting these blatant racist caricatures, Davis does testify to Tom's talent and, in a very minor way at the end, reflect on the tragedy of his life. "The feature of the concerts which was the most painful I have not touched upon," she concedes: "the moments when his master was talking, and Tom was left to himself, – when a weary despair seemed to settle down on the distorted face [of the twelve-year-old], and the stubby little black fingers, wandering over the keys, spoke for Tom's own caged soul within."[29]

The unsigned newspaper description of Blind Tom attributed to Willa Cather thirty years later is not as racist as Davis' account.[30] Here is what appeared in the *Nebraska State Journal* in 1894:

It was a fair audience that gathered at the Lansing last night to listen to Blind Tom. Certainly the man was worth hearing – at least once. Probably there has never been seen on the stage a stranger figure or one more uncanny. He is a human phonograph, a sort of animated memory, with sound producing power. It was a strange sight to see him walk out on the stage and with his own lips – and another man's words – introduce himself and talk quietly about his own idiocy. Then, too, he would applaud himself, and apologize, still in the third person, for his lack of courtesy. There was an insanity, a grotesque horribleness about it that was interestingly unpleasant.

With regard to music, it was wonderful to see what the man could do. It was as if the soul of a Beethoven had slipped into the body of an idiot. In his ears and in his fingers Tom is the peer of some masterful musicians. The movement from the Sonata Pathetique he rendered sympathetically, with real feeling and perception, and the Intermezzo from *Cavalleria Rusticana* was graceful and delicately played, that is, as gracefully as the very unsatisfactory piano would permit. It seems as if Tom were enough afflicted by nature without the additional hindrance of that "upright." The Hungarian Rhapsody No. 2 and Paderewski's "Chant d'Amour" were played with some genius, for certainly that may be called genius which has no basis in intellect.

This was the chief part of the real music. Besides these, Blind Tom played some of his own compositions and gave imitations of storms, banjos, and bagpipes. He offered to repeat, by ear, any piece that anyone in the audience might play. Professor Lichtenstein of the Western Normal came forward and played Gottschalk's "Tremolo," a piece that apparently was a little too difficult for a successful test. Still Tom did much better than one would expect. . . .

Tom is really a wonderfully gifted player. He has a marvelous ear and wonderful delicacy of touch, but these gifts are shut up in the body of an overgrown child. One laughs at the man's queer actions, and yet, after all, the sight is not laughable. It brings us too near to the things that we sane people do not like to think of.[31]

Even if Cather did not write this account – as an older woman she could not remember having seen Blind Tom[32] – she would have known who he was; and his fame was such that he certainly influenced her portrait of d'Arnault.

The pianist Cather was quite conscious of having seen and used as her model for Blind d'Arnault was Blind Boone. As Mildred Bennett explains in *The World of Willa Cather*, Boone made regular visits to Red Cloud and "always stayed at the Holland House where he was treated with every consideration. Mrs. Holland did not go out evenings; and therefore, Boone gave special concerts for her and her guests, who listened eagerly to the heavy black man rocking back and forth constantly, bringing unbelievably sweet melodies from the keyboard."[33] Routinely billed as a second Blind Tom, Boone, like Tom, was blind, black, extraordinarily gifted musically, and blessed with an astounding ability to play by ear. But unlike Tom, Boone was a ragger. Born in 1864 in Missouri, John William Boone was the son of a cook for federal troops and a bugler in the army. He went off as a boy to the St. Louis School for the Blind (townspeople of Warrensburg, Missouri, raised the money), but constantly ran away to play with the ragtime piano players in the "tenderloin" district.

The historian John C. Crighton observes that "these escapades resulted in his being expelled from school, but apparently gave him an introduction to ragtime as played by unknown black musicians pounding away on their upright pianos in bordellos."[34]

There are striking differences between Boone's life and Blind Tom's. Boone's mental capacity was never questioned; he had one manager all of his adult life, John Lange, Jr., a prosperous African American businessman and community leader in Columbia, Missouri; he incorporated into the Blind Boone Concert Company three other black musicians (banjo, violin, and vocalist); and he was heavily influenced in his youth by ragtime. Not least important, he married and, as Crighton says, "attained the status of a comparatively wealthy man."[35] Although his fortunes reversed when audiences shrank after the turn of the century, Boone for a number of years owned a ten-room house he had built in Columbia; and while he chose not to publish his original compositions, preferring to perform them himself, he "cut player piano rolls of some of his ragtime and humorous numbers."[36]

However, despite these differences, Blind Tom and Blind Boone, as musical geniuses who were black men, both had to contend with white racism. In particular, they had to confront the performance expectations created by minstrelsy, virtually the only theatrical venue open to black men in the United States in the nineteenth century. Minstrel tradition caricatured African Americans as servile buffoons or incompetent clowns.[37] What is striking is the contrasting power of the two pianists to resist that stereotyping. Tom, born a slave and either mentally impaired or treated in such a way that his mental capacities seemed limited, was managed by unscrupulous whites who robbed him and, it seems obvious, manipulated his image to ensure that he appear stupid, even subhuman, except for his piano playing. Boone, born fifteen years later, free, and without any real or imagined mental limitations, was handled honestly by a fellow black man and consequently had a career which, if not as well known as Blind Tom's, certainly seems to have been happier. Where Blind Tom was commonly portrayed as a freak – a side-show attraction – testimonials about Boone quoted in his concert programs stress only amazement and praise, calling him "remarkable," "wonderful," "a master."[38] They present Boone as an astonishing, gifted musician, not as an animal. Of course, these testimonials were almost certainly chosen for reprinting by Boone's manager, Lange, or by Boone himself. But that is the point: Boone, unlike Tom, had both the autonomy and, evidently, the kind of manager that allowed him to create positive, dignified images of himself.

Concert performances by artists such as Blind Tom, who died in 1908, and Blind Boone, who died in 1927, disappeared early in the twentieth century. John C. Crighton describes the transition in his discussion of Boone:

> The popularity and success of Boone's programs depended upon the social life of his times. In the 1880s and 1890s the local opera house was the amusement center of most towns. In this hall – as in Columbia's Haden Opera House – there was a weekly succession of entertainment features, such as musical concerts, light operas, comedies, piano recitals and speeches. The piano was the major source of music for middle class families. The girls in these homes spent many hours learning to play the piano, and their parents were willing to pay to hear piano concerts.
>
> However, in the decade of World War I the motion picture and radio were developed, and these satisfied the demand for popular entertainment. Opera houses were transformed into movie theaters. Sophisticated music lovers attended the concert halls to hear such internationally renowned pianists as Paderewski and Rachmaninov. The result was that there was no longer a demand for the sort of musical melange furnished by Boone's company, and few halls where such live performances could be staged.[39]

Crighton's emphasis on piano playing as a trope for middle-class, domestic values in pre–First World War America corresponds to the way in which the warmth, coziness, and domesticity surrounding d'Arnault's piano-playing in *My Ántonia* suggest a supposedly simpler, more innocent time in America than that of Cather's audience, reading as they were during and immediately following World War One.

Historical information about Blind Tom and Blind Boone underscores Blind d'Arnault's realistic function in *My Ántonia*. Although not familiar to most late twentieth-century readers, a fictitious, itinerant, blind, black piano player at the time of the novel's publication evoked an actual figure – particularly Blind Tom, but also Blind Boone, and perhaps others. D'Arnault's presence emphasizes Cather's point that we have journeyed back to premodern America, to a time before movie theaters, when travelling live entertainers provided popular culture and brought communities together in the United States. Rocking at the piano and playing old favorites so that the assembled wayfarers and workers at the "Boys' Home" in Black Hawk can sing and dance, Cather's blind pianist reinforces the book's preservationist mission.

But couldn't all of this be communicated through any travelling artist? Why make d'Arnault black?

* * * * *

My answer is that a black musician erupts as if out of nowhere in *My Ántonia* because he serves to embody the African American cultural presence that has all along been in the text. That is, d'Arnault is simply the outward, visible sign of an invisible presence operating throughout the book.

Overtly, d'Arnault signifies art that is sensual, communal, and full of forbidden pleasure. Arriving in Black Hawk in March, he represents the "one break in the dreary monotony of that month" (181); the black pianist brings warmth and new vitality. He resembles, we are told directly, a fertility god – "some glistening African god of pleasure, full of strong, savage blood" (191). As such, d'Arnault fulfills one of the stereotypic functions of African American characters in white modernist texts. He injects passion and liberating sexual energy into a cold, frozen, white landscape (a literal one in Cather's book) that is afraid of sex. For good reason, we do not see d'Arnault on the concert stage, where he will perform on Monday, but in the hotel called the Boys' Home on Saturday night, where he performs privately and, with Mrs. Gardiner gone, against the rules. It is significant that in Mildred Bennett's memory of Blind Boone's playing at the Holland House, Mrs. Holland was always present (she "did not go out evenings"), while in Cather's novel not only is Mrs. Gardiner out, she is out of town. Assigned the role of making white

73

people feel happy, d'Arnault plays "good old plantation songs" such as imitation black music by white composer Stephen Foster, "My Old Kentucky Home" (184–85). The white men gathered in the warmth of the hotel parlor (while white women hide in the next room) are made to feel relaxed and secure by the sweet, sad, sentimental tunes. "They sang one Negro melody after another, while the mulatto sat rocking himself, his head thrown back, his yellow face lifted, his shrivelled eyelids never fluttering" (185).

What explodes into this cozy, nostalgic space, under the expert fingers of Blind d'Arnault, is sex – both homosexual erotic abandon (behind the closed door) and heterosexual passion (out in the open). "In the middle of a crashing waltz, d'Arnault suddenly began to play softly, and, turning to one of the men who stood behind him, whispered, 'Somebody dancing in there.' He jerked his bullet-head toward the dining-room. 'I hear little feet – girls, I 'spect' " (189). At this point the young women who have been waltzing with each other in secret behind the door (surely one of Cather's most literal images of love in the closet) come out and dance with the men. An evening of joyful, physical ecstasy is facilitated by d'Arnault. "At a word from Kirkpatrick, d'Arnault spread himself out over the piano, and began to draw the dance music out of it, while the perspiration shone on his short wool and on his uplifted face. . . . Whenever the dancers paused to change partners or to catch breath, he would boom out softly, 'Who's that goin' back on me? One of these city gentlemen, I bet! Now, you girls, you ain't goin' to let that floor get cold?' "(191). Discussing music in the novel, Richard Giannone argues: "The Blind d'Arnault passage is the pulsating center of *My Ántonia.*" D'Arnault "is elemental musical sensation itself," containing "interior fire" and representing "sensitivity to the irrational and irreducible in man." His "music signals the awakening of something strong and passionate in Ántonia."[40]

Blind d'Arnault's explicit function in *My Ántonia* is easily named. Fulfilling the standard, racist white fantasy that dark-skinned people's access to sexuality is more "primitive," "abandoned," and "uninhibited," the lone black character in Cather's novel exists to liberate the repressed white people. Although he is granted some self-respect – "Johnnie Gardiner came in, directing Blind d'Arnault – he would never consent to be led" (183) – Cather's racism (via Jim Burden) has the upper hand. A character of genuine genius, as were both of his real-life models, d'Arnault may speak and carry himself with dignity, like Boone, but he is given a plantation history and subhuman physical characteristics, like Blind Tom. That is, although Blind d'Arnault will not allow himself to be led, he nevertheless has forced upon him the standard, stereotypic role of the dark, primitive, animalistic Other – in this case both eroticized (glistening god) and eroticizing (the passionate dancing). Conveniently dependent and emasculated, the black man exists in *My Ántonia* as the totally familiar, stereotypic solution to repressed white sexual fears and anxieties.

Yet he is also a genuine artist. Despite being undercut and caricatured, d'Arnault represents creative genius in *My Ántonia*. The schizophrenia of Cather's representation forces the question: Is his genius insisted upon, even as the stereotype is invoked to undercut it, because there is a level at which the music that Blind d'Arnault visibly introduces into the text also – in a different, hidden, suppressed and therefore denied way – functions invisibly?

Toni Morrison discusses the impact of African American people, culture, history, art and experience on dominant-culture white forms; in particular, she raises the important, long-overdue issue of "the way black people ignite critical moments of discovery or change or emphasis in literature not written by them."[41] She explains in "Unspeakable Things Unspoken: The Afro-American Presence in American Literature" that for her it is the how – even more than the why – of racial erasure in white texts that needs to be examined. As Morrison puts it: "What intellectual feats had to be performed by the author or his critic to erase me from a society seething with my presence, and what effect has that performance had on the work?" She argues that critics must reexamine American literature for "the ways in which the presence of Afro-Americans has shaped the choices, the language, the structure – the meaning of so much American literature. A search, in other words, for the ghost in the machine."[42]

My view is that African American music is one such "ghost in the machine" in *My Ántonia*. We know from the Epilogue to *Sapphira and the Slave Girl* as well as from the presence of Blind d'Arnault in *My Ántonia* that Willa Cather was drawn to African American music. My point so far has been that her perspective on black people was thoroughly infected by her racist attitudes. The point of the rest of my discussion will be the possibility that African American art had a deeper and more profound impact on Cather's art than she knew or could admit.

It has long been obvious to readers and critics that the structure of *My Ántonia* is innovative. The book does not follow the usual Western narrative pattern for a novel – what might be described as linear plot development focused on an individual protagonist and shaped into a progressive sequence of events, customarily tracing the familiar trajectory of exposition, complication, conflict, climax, resolution. *My Ántonia*, instead, is organized in important respects as if it had no dominant plot line. It reads like a series of marginal stories – a composition in a minor key, so to speak. Jim Burden even states in the Introduction that the book "hasn't any form" (he says that the narrative is simply the result of his writing down "pretty much all that her name [Ántonia] recalls to me") (iii), although, of course, the book does have form. It is just that the form is unusual. Susan Rosowski describes it as "two major movements, followed by fusion."[43] Judith Fryer finds it made up of "parts" that "have a semi-independent existence of their own, like separate stories."[44] Or as Richard Giannone suggests in *Music in Willa Cather* – though he and I finally differ – we might think about the book's structure by musical analogy.[45]

In *The Making of Jazz*, James Lincoln Collier describes what is believed to be one of the principal features of pre-twentieth-century African American music as its "arrhythmic patches of melody . . . cast in the rough shape of the three-over-two pattern so common to African music."[46] It is not a matter of "African devices pasted onto a European music," Collier explains; rather, "this black music was a true fusion of African and European systems" (23–24). As such, it attempted "to reproduce in the European system implications of the old cross-rhythms of Africa" (24). One result is a different construction of time from that privileged in Western culture. "One contemporary report says, 'One noticeable thing about their [African American] boat-songs was that they seemed often to be sung just a trifle behind time.' . . . Other witnesses have remarked on melodies being 'out of time' " (24). While acknowledging the problem created by the absence of accurate transcriptions from early periods, Collier argues that it is possible on the basis of what we do have – descriptions, some transcriptions, blues and jazz tradition, and recordings made in the 1930s and 1940s – to reconstruct the formal properties of traditional African American music. I think his description has fascinating resonance for the way *My Ántonia* works structurally.

In traditional African American music, Collier explains:

The singers were, at least in portions of their melodies, breaking away from the time framework of the ground beat to produce lines that were essentially rhythmically free. A phrase would not necessarily begin on a beat, or halfway between two beats as in European syncopation, but at some odd point irrelevant to the time scheme, and the remaining notes of the phrase would be equally unleashed from ground beats and meter. The old game of sidewalk cracks and squares comes to mind: in European music the singer steps firmly in the center of the squares, or syncopates by stepping on the cracks; but in this early black music the singer was skipping helter-skelter down the sidewalk, as if cracks and squares did not exist. (24)

As Mikhail Bakhtin has argued, the very nature of the novel is rule-breaking, formal rebellion.[47] Why couldn't a writer skip helter-skelter down the path of memory, ignoring the cracks and squares of conventional novelistic form, as if they did not exist?

Evident in the narrative organization of *My Ántonia* are several of the basic structural principles that Collier theorizes must have governed nineteenth-century (and earlier) African American music, and that Cather might very well have been exposed to in the vernacular black music of her childhood Virginia as well as later as an adult, when the same patterns were finding widespread new expression in ragtime, in the blues, and in the beginnings of jazz. The concepts of arrhythmic patches of melody, of being "out of time," of developing song through cross-rhythms, and of creating lines that break away from a foundation to become rhythmically free all translate narratively into structural features found in *My Ántonia*.

Emphatically not organized by a tight linear plot line, Cather's novel does move forward in a time-removed way, with part of itself seeming to happen slightly behind itself. Beginning with the opening frame, which stages the idea of complex negotiations of time-frames and framing itself, the book resists clean, unitary, forward motion in favor of an almost dreamlike, enveloping constant in which past, present, and future participate. Similarly the notion of Cather's book taking shape through cross-rhythms – Jim's story, Ántonia's story, Lena's, Tiny's – is provocative. And if we think of the Lena Lingard section, for example, we can see the novel as a composition containing narrative lines that break away from the foundation to become structurally free. Most obvious, however, is the way that *My Ántonia* includes arrhythmic patches of story – Peter and Pavel's wedding tale, the tramp's death. These stories within the story set up free-floating narratives and tonalities within the whole that interrupt – create counterpoint – yet are part of the narrative. Collier describes how black musicians in the United States brought not the practice but the *principle* of African cross-rhythm into American music: They "found a new way to express it by standing a melody line apart from the ground beat that ostensibly supported it."[48] Rhythmically – structurally – the multiple stories and patches of story in *My Ántonia* might be thought of as the melody line(s) standing apart from (at various distances at various times) the ground beat of Jim Burden's (and through him, Willa Cather's) remembered life on the Nebraska prairie in the late nineteenth century.

It is important not to overstate this musical analogy. Indeed, my point is that if African American music is present in Cather's novel beyond the literal representation of Blind d'Arnault, it is present as a "ghost"; it operates secretly, invisibly – as a denied presence in the work. But I do think the ghost is there. The structural patterning of the book creates an arrhythmic design that, like traditional black music in the United States and its echoes in ragtime, both performs and constitutes an alternative to elite Western aesthetic principles. Blind d'Arnault's appearance in *My Ántonia* betrays the fact that African American music is crucial to Cather's story, even as her racist descriptions undercut the black artist's importance – render him alien, grotesque, repulsive. In part, this is simply racism: D'Arnault is black, Cather is bigoted, so the portrait is skewed. But also at work, I am saying, is something more complex. The pianist has to be black because he is the visible sign of the invisible black presence in *My Ántonia* that Cather, even if she tried, could not keep out: the novel's structural refusal to reproduce elite, dominant-culture, aesthetic principles; its formal borrowing from an African American aesthetic which mixes Western and nonwestern modes and modalities.

The contemporary black composer T. J. Anderson describes ragtime, the African American music heard everywhere in the United States when Willa Cather was young and the music specifically played by the model she acknowledged for d'Arnault, Blind Boone, as uniquely American. Ragtime, in Anderson's description, results from playing with a German left hand and an African right hand. It is the New World in one, new, perfect, musical gesture.[49] My suggestion is that when Willa Cather, for whom music was the highest art, set out to tell what was for her the quintessentially American story of Ántonia, she echoed in her book's form – in spite of herself – the quintessentially American music that shaped her as an artist, the vernacular black music of her childhood in Virginia and the ragtime of her young adulthood. Her schizophrenic representation of d'Arnault tells us that Cather, like most racist white artists in the United States, wished to deny her debt to African American culture. In the form of the book, however, lives the ghost in the machine.

NOTES

1. "Negro Music," *The Crisis* 1 (February 1911): 12.
2. Willa Cather, *My Ántonia* (Boston: Houghton Mifflin, 1918), p. 184. Page references in the text are to this edition.
3. See Blanche H. Gelfant, "The Forgotten Reaping-Hook: Sex in *My Ántonia*," *American Literature* 43 (1971): 60–82; Richard Giannone, *Music in Willa Cather's Fiction* (Lincoln: University of Nebraska Press, 1968), pp. 116–22; Evelyn Hemick, "The Mysteries of Ántonia," *Willa Cather's My Ántonia*, ed. Harold Bloom (New York:

Chelsea House, 1987), pp. 109–10; and Mike Fischer, "Pastoralism and Its Discontents: Willa Cather and the Burden of Imperialism," *Mosaic* 23 (Winter 1990): 42.

4. For a book-length discussion, see Giannone.

5. For discussion of Cather's use of men rather than women to typify the artist in this novel, and frequently elsewhere, see Sharon O'Brien, *Willa Cather: The Emerging Voice* (New York: Oxford University Press, 1987); Josephine Donovan, *After the Fall: The Demeter-Persephone Myth in Wharton, Cather, and Glasgow* (University Park: Penn State University Press, 1989); and Elizabeth Ammons, *Conflicting Stories: American Women Writers at the Turn into the Twentieth Century* (New York: Oxford University Press, 1991).

6. There are a number of discussions of Jim Burden's limitations as narrator. See, e.g., William J. Stuckey, "*My Ántonia*: A Rose for Miss Cather," *Studies in the Novel* 4 (Fall 1972): 473–83; Judith Fetterley, "*My Ántonia*, Jim Burden and the Dilemma of the Lesbian Writer," *Gender Studies: New Directions in Feminist Criticism*, ed. Judith Specter (Bowling Green: Bowling Green State University Press, 1986), pp. 43–59; and Susan Rosowski, *The Voyage Perilous: Willa Cather's Romanticism* (Lincoln: University of Nebraska Press, 1986), Chapter 6. In contrast, Giannone discusses Jim as a reliable narrator and as an artist capable of celebrating Ántonia (p. 118).

7. See O'Brien, p. 24.

8. Willa Cather, *Sapphira and the Slave Girl* (New York: Knopf, 1940; rpt. Random House, 1975), p. 281.

9. O'Brien, p. 44.

10. I discuss the racism of *Sapphira and the Slave Girl* in detail in *Conflicting Stories*, Chapter 8. See also Toni Morrison's views in *Playing in the Dark: Whiteness and the Literary Imagination* (Cambridge: Harvard University Press, 1992).

11. Cather's stereotypic views of Asian Americans appear in two short stories, "The Conversion of Sum Loo" and "A Son of the Celestial," *Willa Cather's Collected Short Fiction, 1892–1912*, ed. Virginia Faulkner (Lincoln: University of Nebraska Press, 1965). Discussion of her treatment of Mexicans, Indians, and Jews can be found in E. A. Mares, "Padre Martinez, Defender of the People," *New Mexico Magazine* (June 1985): 57–60; Fischer, "Pastoralism and Its Discontents"; and Loretta Wasserman, "Cather's Semitism," *Cather Studies* 2 (1993): 1–22. Also, in addition to *Conflicting Stories*, I discuss her racism in "Cather and the New Canon: 'The Old Beauty' and the Issue of the Empire," *Cather Studies* 3 (1996): 256–66.

12. W. E. B. Du Bois, "The Negro in Literature and Art," *Annals of the American Academy of Political and Social Science*, 49 (September 1913): 237; rpt. *Writings by W. E. B. Du Bois in Periodicals Edited by Others*, ed. Herbert Aptheker, vol. 2 (Millwood, NY: Kraus-Thomson Organization Limited, 1982), p. 91.

13. Sui Sin Far, *Mrs. Spring Fragrance* (Chicago: A. C. McClurg & Co., 1912), p. 22 (emphasis mine).

14. Austin, *Earth Horizon* (Cambridge, MA: Houghton Mifflin, 1932), p. 359.

15. Rayford W. Logan, *The Negro in the United States: A Brief History* (Princeton, NJ: D. Van Nostrand Co., 1957), p. 39.

16. Winfield H. Collins, *The Truth About Lynching and The Negro in the South, In Which the Author Pleads That the South Be Made Safe for the White Race* (New York: Neale Publishing Co., 1918), pp. 72–73.

17. See, e.g., Ida B. Wells, *Southern Horrors: Lynch Law in All Its Phases* (1892); Anna Julia Cooper, *A Voice from the South* (1892); W. E. B. Du Bois, *The Souls of Black Folk* (1903); or Herbert J. Seligmann, *The Negro Faces America* (1920). For an overview of thinking during the period, see Thomas F. Gossett, *Race: The History of an Idea* (Dallas: Southern Methodist University Press, 1963).

18. Theodore Drury, "The Negro in Classic Music; Or, Leading Opera, Oratorio and Concert Singers," *The Colored American Magazine* 5 (Sept. 1902), 324.

19. Robert W. Carter, "Opera and the Afro-American Artist," *The Colored American Magazine* 5 (June 1902): 143.

20. Ibid., p. 143; and Carter, "The Drury Opera Company in Verdi's 'Aida,' " *The Colored American Magazine* 6 (August 1903): 597.

21. Sarah A. Allen (a penname used by Hopkins), "Mr. M. Hamilton Hodges," *The Colored American Magazine* 7 (March 1904): 167.

22. James Lincoln Collier, *The Making of Jazz: A Comprehensive History* (Boston: Houghton Mifflin, 1978), pp. 43–44. Also useful is Eileen Southern's overview, *The Music of Black Americans: A History* (New York: W. W. Norton, 1971). For description of ragtime by a musician and fiction writer during the same period as Cather, see James Weldon Johnson, *The Autobiography of an Ex-Coloured Man* (1912) in *Three Negro Classics*, ed. John Hope Franklin (New York: Avon, 1965), pp. 447–49.

23. See James Woodress, *Willa Carter: A Literary Life* (Lincoln: University of Nebraska Press, 1987), p. 291; or Mildred R. Bennett, *The World of Willa Carter* (Lincoln: University of Nebraska Press, 1961), p. 155.

24. James M. Trotter, *Music and Some Highly Musical People: Containing Brief Chapters on I. A Description of Music. II. The Music of Nature. III. A Glance at the History of Music. IV. The Power, Beauty, and Uses of Music. Following Which Are Given Sketches of the Lives of Remarkable Musicians of the Colored Race. With Portraits, And An Appendix Containing Copies of Music Composed by Colored Men* (Boston: Lee and Shepard, and New York: Charles T. Dillingham, 1881), pp. 141–42, 143–44.

25. Geneva H. Southall, *Blind Tom: The Post-Civil War Enslavement of a Black Musical Genius*, Book I (Minneapolis: Challenge Productions, 1979), p. 73.

26. Geneva Southall, "Blind Tom: A Misrepresented and Neglected Composer-Pianist," *The Black Perspective in Music* 3 (May 1975): 146. Also see Geneva H. Southall, *The Continuing Enslavement of Blind Tom, The Black Pianist-Composer (1865–1887)*, Book II (Minneapolis: Challenge Productions, 1983). A third and final volume is forthcoming.

27. See Southall, "Blind Tom," p. 142 her books I and II, passim; and Anna Amalie Tutein, "The Phenomenon of 'Blind Tom,' " *Etude* (February 1918): pp. 91–92.

28. Southall, *Blind Tom*, Book I, p. 73.

29. Rebecca Harding Davis, "Blind Tom," *Atlantic Monthly* 10 (November 1862): 580, 581, 584, 585.

30. It is possible that this unsigned review was not written by Cather. Its attribution to her by William Curtin was made on the basis of biographical and internal evidence (author's conversations with William Curtin, summer 1992), neither of which can be conclusive.

31. *Nebraska State Journal* (May 18, 1894), p. 6; quoted in William Curtin, ed., *The World and the Parish: Willa Cather's Articles and Reviews, 1893–1902* (Lincoln: University of Nebraska Press, 1970), vol. 1, pp. 166–67. The deleted paragraph, for which I am grateful to William Curtin, reads:

    Other features were musical spelling, analysis of chords, and the phonetic spelling and pronunciation of "Transmagnificanubandantiality." There was also an imitation of Stephen A. Douglas and an original poem on "The Man That Sprained His Hnee" [*sic*], and a little idyl telling how Tom "Said good-bye to the hotel clerk and he fell against the wall."

32. Bennett, p. 248.

33. Bennett, p. 155.

34. John C. Crighton, " 'Blind' Boone/Early Link to Ragtime," *The Columbia Daily Tribune*, Columbia, MO, October 20, 1974, p. 13. For providing me with information about Blind Boone, I am very grateful to Professor Susan Rosowski at the University of Nebraska and to the Nebraska State Historical Society in Lincoln, Nebraska.
35. Crighton, p. 13.
36. Ibid.
37. See Gary D. Engle, *This Grotesque Essence: Plays from the American Minstrel Stage* (Baton Rouge: Louisiana State University Press, 1978).
38. Testimonials accompanying the concert program for the M. E. Church, University Place, Sat. Evening Jan. 20, '06. Courtesy of the Nebraska State Historical Society, Lincoln, Nebraska.
39. Crighton, p. 13.
40. Giannone, pp. 120, 118, 119.
41. Morrison, *Playing in the Dark*, p. viii.
42. Toni Morrison, "Unspeakable Things Unspoken: The Afro-American Presence in American Literature," *Michigan Quarterly Review* 28 (Winter 1989): 12, 11.
43. Rosowski, p. 76.
44. Judith Fryer, *Felicitous Space: The Imaginative Structures of Edith Wharton and Willa Cather* (Chapel Hill: University of North Carolina Press, 1986), p. 274.
45. See Giannone, pp. 107ff.
46. Collier, p. 24.
47. See *The Dialogic Imagination: Four Essays by M. M. Bakhtin*, ed. Michael Holquist (Austin, TX: University of Texas Press, 1981).
48. Collier, p. 25.
49. Conversation with the composer, spring 1991.

4

Displacing Dixie: The Southern Subtext in *My Ántonia*

ANNE GOODWYN JONES

> Two by two and three by three
> Missouri lies by Tennessee;
> Row on row, an hundred deep,
> Maryland and Georgia sleep;
> Wistfully the poplars sigh
> Where Virginia's thousands lie.
> – Willa Cather, "The
> Namesake" (1902)

> Row after row with strict impunity
> The headstones yield their names to the element,
> The wind whirrs without recollection . . .
> – Allen Tate, "Ode to the Confederate
> Dead" (1928, 1937)

Yet I found curious survivals; some of the figures of my old life seemed to be waiting for me in the new.
– Willa Cather, *My Ántonia* (1918)

M OST readers rightly think of Willa Cather as a novelist of prairies and mesas, of Middle West and Southwest. Cather herself inscribed a friend's copy of *O Pioneers!* with the note saying that she had "hit the home pasture" with this novel of the plains.[1] The work of her major middle period, which many think her best work, and which includes *My Ántonia*, is clearly Western. The University of Nebraska Press has published collections of her work; Red Cloud, Nebraska, hosts Cather conferences; and reportedly USA Network was to film *My Ántonia* on location in Nebraska.

I am grateful to Sharon O'Brien for her always helpful suggestions. She and my colleague David Leverenz have been ideal readers, and I thank them both.

85

So what is a poem honoring the Confederate dead doing in the Cather repertoire? Like Allen Tate's much more famous "Ode," Cather's poem shows us row upon row of Confederate gravestones, trees rustled by wind, "names" of soldiers and their states, and a solitary meditative narrator contemplating the meanings of the Civil War Southern dead.[2] Why would a lover of the West, of open space and red grass, of movement and the future – and of the active, vital Bohemian immigrant Ántonia Shimerda – picture herself enclosed in a static southern cemetery, surrounded by the past, beside the grave of a rebel soldier?

Was Willa Cather a closet Confederate?

As a closet lesbian, critics have argued, Cather developed strategies for telling her sexual story in code.[3] Reading coded stories is risky, challenging, and fun: it is also dead serious, for coded texts typically avoid direct speech for good reason – to communicate safely and selectively. As early as 1980, feminist critics Sandra Gilbert and Susan Gubar claimed that women writers, whatever their sexuality, wrote coded texts, closeting their anger, for example, in "palimpsestic" texts or displacing it onto minor but disruptive figures like *Jane Eyre*'s Bertha Mason.[4] Even earlier, W. E. B. DuBois observed that African Americans had a "double consciousness"; their texts deliberately coded resistant messages in language that could pass as docile.[5] In each case – homosexual desire, female anger, black resistance – a voice muted by the fear and caution that history has taught speaks in code through a dominant idiom, "passing" through master narratives. Perhaps Cather had good reason not to speak forthrightly of her Southern past, as well as of her sexuality, for most of her life. And perhaps we can decode some of her Southern speech, and some of her reasons for disguising its dialect, in a new regional reading of *My Ántonia*.

When Willa Cather wrote that she had "hit the home pasture" in writing about Nebraska, she neglected to mention a crucial fact: her home pasture was, until the age of nine, the hills of Virginia, not the plains of Nebraska. Cather spent her childhood as a member of a privileged Southern family in Winchester in the Shenandoah Valley. By the time she moved to Nebraska, she knew every nook and cranny of the Virginia house (Willow Shade), the trails in the woods, the blue haze of the mountains. She knew mountain people and their stories; she had absorbed the etiquette of race relations and seen and heard the intimate lives of African Americans; she had learned her station in a deeply hierarchical social world. In every sense of the word, then, she knew her place.

She knew her place, but she did not always keep it. A family story tells of the time a venerable visiting judge ' "strok[ed] her curls and talk[ed] to her in the playful platitudes one addressed to little girls.' "[6] But, Sharon O'Brien continues, she "refused to employ the playful platitudes with which little girls were supposed to flatter Southern gentlemen." Instead, she shouted, " 'I'se a dang'ous nigger, I is!' " By renaming herself thus, crossing race and probably gender and age boundaries, she defied both the name and the namer – a white man – of "little girls." It was the act of a writer.

Despite its constraints, leaving that home pasture would be enormously painful for Cather as a child. Clearly the world split in two for her then, at age nine, just as starkly as it would again for her "about 1922."[7] The world before 1883 was Virginia; after that, Red Cloud. Here is part of her 1913 description of that loss in a newspaper interview:

I shall never forget my introduction to [Nebraska]. . . . As we drove further and further out into the country, I felt a good deal as if we had come to the end of everything – it was a kind of erasure of personality.

I would not know how much a child's life is bound up in the woods and hills and meadows around it, if I had not been jerked away from all these and thrown out into a country as bare as a piece of sheet iron. I had heard my father say you had to show grit in a new country, and I would have got on pretty well during that ride if it had not been for the larks. Every now and then one flew up and sang a few splendid notes and dropped down into the grass again. That reminded me of something – I don't know what, but my one purpose in life just then was not to cry, and every time they did it, I thought I should go under.

For the first week or two on the homestead [her grandparents' home eighteen miles from Red Cloud] I had that kind of contraction of the stomach which comes from homesickness. I didn't like canned things anyhow, and I made an agreement with myself that I would not eat much until I got back to Virginia and could get some fresh mutton.[8]

According to James Woodress, "even Old Vic, the sheep dog . . . was given to a neighbor. Willa remembered [that] just as the family was about to board the train at Back Creek, the old dog broke loose and came running across the fields dragging her chain. Young Willa felt that it was more than she could bear."[9] The pain and helplessness that Cather felt at the lost of Old Vic, and at the rising and singing and then falling of the larks, somehow summarized the pain of the complex loss she had to undergo with the move, a loss that was geographical, social, cultural, familial, and personal. It was a loss that at first seemed to leave nothing in its stead. And it was a loss that would require deep grieving to free her to find a new world to love.

Like Cather, Jim Burden was around ten when he was removed from his home, his countryside, and his culture and taken to live in Nebraska. Cather describes her own move as an "erasure of personality"; Jim says "I felt erased, blotted out."[10] She describes her new landscape as "bare as a piece of sheet iron"; Jim calls it "not a country at all, but the material out of which countries are made." As we will see later, Cather says her grandmother's rattlesnake cane was the first thing to suggest the new land might not be so "flat" after all; when Jim's grandmother carries her rattlesnake cane with her on Jim's first visit to the garden, Jim feels for the first time "entirely happy" (18).

Yet whereas the young Cather traveled west with her mother, father, three younger siblings, a grandmother, and two young cousins, as well as the family maid, both of Jim's parents are dead – recently dead – and he travels only with Jake Marpole, a family "hand." His home will be with two aging grandparents whom he does not even recognize. If Cather experienced the move as a traumatic loss, and if it took her a long time to grieve, it is odd that Jim Burden is virtually never homesick after the visit to the garden, seems to have practically no memories of Virginia, and rarely mentions even his parents. After informing us of the reasons for his move and describing his traumatic night ride into an entirely new life, Jim moves on to the story that he wants to tell (or so he

has told the "Willa Cather" of the Introduction), the story of Nebraska and of "his" Ántonia. Caught up in locating the meaning
of life there, he spends little time describing the past that preceded
his Nebraska past or the process of transition. It is tempting to conclude then that Cather's *My Ántonia* as well as Jim's "My Ántonia"
is about Ántonia and Nebraska, not Jim Burden, much less the
people and culture Jim left behind in Virginia, or the difficult passage from his first life to his second. Indeed, this is what many
critics and readers have concluded. Can we, though, find traces of
the South troubling the Midwestern terrain of *My Ántonia*? Does
Jim not grieve his losses? Are there no figures from his past to
haunt the present? If not, how can we understand what comes to
seem an emotional misstep, a deliberate erasure, on Cather's part
as his author?

Cather made her autobiographical statement (quoted above)
in 1913, as an adult, years after her move, just as Jim does as the
fictional adult author of "My Ántonia." Yet as we have seen, the
two narrators represent loss and grief very differently. Instead of
grieving, Jim as a ten-year-old has dealt with his loss as children
his age frequently do: by pushing it down and aside, waiting for
a time when he will be better able to feel and come to terms with
the pain. Yet whereas Cather as an adult is able to remember her
pain, the adult Jim can experience grief only as an observer, by
recalling and narrating the stories of others who grieved in various ways. Mr. Shimerda's mourning turns to melancholy, and
he commits suicide; Ántonia, on the other hand, vividly recol-
lects her home in Europe, experiences the pain of loss that these
recollections elicit, and moves on to engage in a new life in a
new world.

Displacing his losses onto other figures costs Jim dearly. Ántonia has told her own stories; thus she has been able to recover
the past and to let it go. By the end of the novel, she is fully
engaged with new people in a new life in a new land. Jim, by
contrast, has reverted to his past. His marriage has failed; his New
York job is in the law office of a friend of his mother's (one of
the few times she is even mentioned); and he seeks to return to
boyhood when he returns – and plans to return again and again
– to Ántonia as one of "Cuzak's boys," a surrogate son. We must

infer that Jim, like Mr. Shimerda, has not been able to let go. Even his effort to return to the "incommunicable past" (238) in writing this story, "My Ántonia," will fail to communicate directly the memories that are most deeply troubling to him, since he displaces them onto others and replaces their loss with the loss of Ántonia. In short, Jim buries his oldest memories in an almost indecipherable code.

By contrast, Cather was able to tell her own stories; by the end of her writing career Cather had written explicitly about Virginia in her fiction. In what is arguably the most innovative of her fictions in some respects, *Sapphira and the Slave Girl* (1940), Cather breaks the boundary between fiction and memoir by inserting into this novel her first person autobiographical self. It is possible, however, to trace the hidden contours of Jim's – and Cather's – missing past throughout the text of *My Ántonia*. In doing so we can find "unwritten, cancelled Virginias" embedded in the text of this Nebraska novel, if we know how to decode the signs and read the palimpsestic traces.[11]

Pressed to locate something distinctively Southern in *My Ántonia*, contemporary readers may think first of the story of Blind d'Arnault. This Southern black musician's life – especially Jim's telling of it – appears to typify Southern racial practices. Raised on a plantation where "the spirit if not the fact of slavery persisted," d'Arnault is the deformed child of the family laundress (119). Drawn to the music he hears from a Big House piano, he blindly seeks it out and – in Jim Burden's words – "found his way to the Thing, to its mouth. He touched it softly, and it answered softly, kindly. He shivered and stood still. Then he began to feel it all over, ran his fingertips along the slippery sides, embraced the carved legs. . . . He approached this highly artificial instrument through a mere instinct, and coupled himself to it, as if he knew it was to piece him out and make a whole creature of him" (120). Jim's Victorian assumptions linking blacks to sensuality, and sensuality to "animal desires" (121), certainly are consistent with Southern discourse. And in case we missed the point, those assumptions are spelled out with utter clarity elsewhere in Jim's story. "[D'Arnault] could never learn like other people, never acquired any finish. He was always a Negro prodigy who played barbarously and wonderfully. As piano-playing it was perhaps abominable, but as music it was something real, vitalized by a sense of rhythm. . . ." In Black Hawk, he looks "like some glistening African god of pleasure, full of strong, savage blood" (121).

Unfortunately, such assumptions, though consistent with the South, were by no means exclusive to it. Racist discourse of this sort pervaded the nation during the early twentieth century. Cather could be confident that, far from offending her white non-Southern readers, she was speaking their language. In fact, she has Jim insert a detail that was likely to be too liberal for some of those readers, when Jim notes that Blind d'Arnault "spent Saturday and Sunday at our comfortable hotel." Segregation was of course *de jure*, the law in the Jim Crow South; yet it was *de facto* the practice and the preference across the country. This textual representation of integration thus would have carried a charge of social meaning no longer experienced by readers today.

But the traces of the South are clearest neither in Jim's rendition of Victorian racist discourse, nor in his approving observation of change. They appear instead in his personal, private response to the sight and sound of d'Arnault, and in the early memories they stir up. "It was the soft, amiable Negro voice, like those I remembered from early childhood, with the note of docile subservience in it. He had the Negro head, too; almost no head at all, nothing behind the ears but folds of neck under close-clipped wool. He would have been repulsive if his face had not been so kindly and happy. It was the happiest face I had seen since I left Virginia" (118). In this remarkable passage Jim seems to hope to convey not so much his racist repugnance but what he believes humanizes the otherwise repellent voice and face: amiability, docility, happiness. In the South, especially, the reward for staying in one's place, for docility, was supposed to be happiness. The kind white "mistress" who helps d'Arnault when he is a child exemplifies this paternalistic ideology. Jim thus believes he is confronting and decoding a familiar figure, whose happiness means that he knows and accepts his place. Readers would have to wait for Quentin Compson, in Faulkner's *The*

Sound and the Fury, to find a white boy who could see how Jim's "perceptions" might well reach only as deep as d'Arnault's superlatively performed surface.[12]

For our purposes, what is interesting is not the truth of Jim's representation of d'Arnault but what it reveals of himself as a Southerner. The ambivalence of his descriptions – d'Arnault is repulsive but kindly, brainless but amiable, sensual but subservient – testifies to the contradictory Southern blend of abstract racist theory and actual human relationships, of paternalism and intimacy.

Jim's response to Blind d'Arnault is more, then, than that of a simple observer. D'Arnault stirs up in Jim old issues of relationship and identity based on Southern experience. In a new context, however, the relational possibility of identification with d'Arnault – a possibility both invoked and forbidden by southern social rigidity – threatens to lead Jim to blur once-clear cultural boundaries between the races by seeing himself in this figure from his past. Such troubling of supposedly fixed categories shapes the very structure of the chapter.

In a recent essay, Richard Millington has claimed that *My Ántonia* "can best be described as a contest between two kinds of narrative," the oral story and the written novel.[13] Using Walter Benjamin's essay from *Illuminations*, "The Storyteller," to develop the distinction, Millington argues that stories told orally are, unlike novels, social, intimate, embodied experiences; for both tellers and listeners they offer the " 'presence of voice.' "[14] Millington shows that Cather defeats the novel's generic collusion with middle-class values and individualized subjectivity by writing a novel that consists of stories. For Millington, Jim's joyful desire to become one of "Cuzak's boys" at the end is unhealthy only if we accept the (generic) novel's requirement of middle-class "maturity." From the point of view of the (generic) story, however, it is an "anti-ending" to a "counter-novel" in which "book and character alike break free of middle-class culture's master narrative of maturity, normalcy, and health."[15]

The American South – it is almost a cliché – is a region where oral storytelling has never died. Images of sitting on the porch (or in a darkened room) "telling lies" to one another pervade the fiction of Southerners black and white, female and male, from Zora Neale Hurston to William Faulkner, from Lee Smith to Ernest Gaines. It makes sense then to see Cather's preference as part of her Southern heritage. But historicizing Millington's argument will also deflate its liberatory utopianism. If telling stories had resulted in "breaking free" of master narratives, the South would have been a very different place. Instead of producing liberation, storytelling can offer a temporary and thus conservative "escape valve" for resistance and for the hope of freedom. It would not be hard to argue that such has been the history of all sorts of storytelling in the South. What sort of story does Jim tell, then, in Chapter VII of "The Hired Girls"?

The d'Arnault chapter opens with a confident narrative voice making a magisterial claim: "Winter lasts too long in country towns" (116). Blind d'Arnault then makes his entrance into the narrative represented only as an evening's entertainment for Jim and other bored white boys and men, a "break in the dreary monotony" of March.

This would have been the comfortable way for Cather's readers to contain the meanings of a black musician: to represent him as a paid entertainer for white males who thus maintain control. Yet in what follows Jim gives a richer rendering of d'Arnault than such a containment should allow, a rendering that opens the door to serious art as well as popular entertainment, black agency as well as white power, and women's presence as well as men's. Thus the story that Jim frames as a break in winter's monotony becomes a story about Southern racial relations; a story whose narrating voice opens in full control ends with a voice that has nearly lost it. We have seen hints of trouble to the master narrative of white male control in Jim's startling rendering of d'Arnault's relation to the piano as a sexual body: luxuriating in sensual detail, Jim's story itself hints that he may identify with d'Arnault at some level. Trouble continues when d'Arnault instigates a breach in the gender divide at this all-male party in Black Hawk. Sensing the presence of women in the dining room next door ("'I hear little feet – girls, I'spect.'" [121]), he encourages them to come in and dance with the men. For d'Arnault, it is an interesting revision of a childhood story told

93

on the same page: the traumatic entrance of his white mistress Miss Nellie into the room where he was playing the piano, the very piano Jim has rendered so sensually. While d'Arnault gains more control in this version, for Jim, d'Arnault's invitation to the women forces a revision of the containment and control with which Jim began his story.

And for Cather, it allows a chapter that began with a confident white male voice and a master narrative to end in sexual uncertainty. The sexual disturbance has been provoked not only by d'Arnault's agency, but also by Jim's – and white culture's – understanding of "blackness." Thus although the potential for racial disturbance is muted – d'Arnault "taps his way upstairs, after bowing to everybody, docile and happy" (123), just as Jim remembers Virginia black folk – the potential for sexual disturbance stimulated by the meanings of "blackness" begins to speak. Jim walks home with Ántonia. Both are "so excited that we dreaded to go to bed"; their solution is to whisper "in the cold until the restlessness was slowly chilled out of us" (123). Given the association of d'Arnault, the piano, music, and dancing – blackness – with sexuality, this passage asks to be read as a scene of unacknowledged sexual desire.

The choice of "dread" complicates this reading, however. Dread is not a simple reluctance to part company or even a suppression of desire. It is an intense fear. Is this dread then a fear of separation? of sexual desire? of sexual acts, "going to bed?" A close and careful look at the traces of the South in *My Ántonia* will bring us closer to some answers. For the time being, we will simply note that Cather, through Jim, ends the chapter with an uncertainty – somehow associated with blackness, art, women, sexuality, and Jim's momentarily revived Virginia past – that subverts the confidence associated with white masculinity and master narratives with which it began. Subverts it, that is, until the "restlessness was slowly chilled out of us" (123).

As a young poet and novelist, Cather had dealt with the rupture of her childhood first by heroicizing the Virginia past – as she does in her early poem "The Namesake," published in 1903 – and then by apparently abandoning the subject of the South altogether. So successfully did the novelist bury the pain of losing her childhood home that most Cather readers would probably agree with critic Susan Rosowski that "Willa Cather's confrontation with the land *began* [my emphasis] when she was nine years old and moved with her family from Virginia to Nebraska."[16] Yet her confrontation with the land had begun, in her life and her writing, with Virginia. And it was to that land that she would return near the end of both her life and her writing. As we saw, Cather's last and most openly autobiographical novel, *Sapphira and the Slave Girl*, is set in her childhood home in Virginia, Willow Shade.

Jim too writes – he writes "My Ántonia" itself – as a way of constructing meanings for the past. Indeed, from the very outset of the novel, he uses images of writing and erasure to come to terms with his Nebraska past. But Jim uses writing differently, less directly. He introduces Ántonia, for example, not as *herself*, but as a "central *figure* [my emphasis]" of his life. This word, which we have already seen in the later phrase "figures of my old life," suggests both a person and a form of representation, a trope. The "Cather" of the Introduction also uses Ántonia in this way: "this girl seemed to *mean to us* [my emphasis] the country, the conditions, the whole adventure of our childhood." As if to underline the point, Jim tells "Cather" in New York that he has written down all that Ántonia's *"name"* [my emphasis] recalls to him. And he writes "across the *face* [my emphasis]" of the portfolio the words "My Ántonia," naming her so that she (that is, her name, her character) will speak only her meanings to him, so that she will be only *his* Ántonia. Perhaps, more humbly, Jim simply recognizes the limits of his own project. But in either case, appropriation or acknowledgment, it is clear that both Jim and "Cather" make no claims to represent Ántonia's own truth. And as if to emphasize its role as signifier, when Ántonia's name first appears in Jim's memoir, it is footnoted.

Unlike Willa Cather, Jim uses writing to repress the old and replace it with the new. At one point, for example, Jim identifies Ántonia's as the face that lies "at the very bottom" of his memory (322). How can this be so, when he had known his own mother's face for his first nine years? It can be so only through narrative acts of rewriting, repression, and displacement. Despite

Jim's displacements, however, the past leaks through, as we saw with the story of Blind d'Arnault and as we shall now see in another story that seems, for obscure reasons, important to Jim. It takes place in the basement of Jim's grandparents' house after Mr. Shimerda's suicide, at Christmas. In it, Mr. Shimerda's ghost appears to Jim; and in this scene we see another cluster of rare references to Virginia.

Jim is deeply moved by Mr. Shimerda's death, moved in ways that the text alone does not fully explain. Sitting alone in the kitchen, he meditates on the dead man, convincing himself that Mr. Shimerda's spirit is abiding with him in the only place where he had seemed "content." To Jim, Mr. Shimerda's hair

made him look like the old portraits I remembered in Virginia. . . . I knew it was homesickness that had killed Mr. Shimerda, and I wondered whether his released spirit would not eventually find its way back to his own country. I thought of how far it was to Chicago, and then to Virginia, to Baltimore – and then the great wintry ocean. No . . . surely, his exhausted spirit . . . was resting now in this quiet house.

I was not frightened but I made no noise . . . [when I] went down to the kitchen . . . There . . . I thought and thought about Mr. Shimerda. . . . I went over all that Ántonia had ever told me about his life before he came to this country . . . such vivid pictures came to me they might have been Mr. Shimerda's memories, not yet faded out from the air in which they had haunted him. . . . I believed he had been in that very kitchen all afternoon, on his way back to his own country . . . he had only been so unhappy that he could not live any longer. (54–67 *passim*)

Especially striking here are the scene's echoes of the first chapter. There Jim had said his parents' spirits were looking for him at home in Virginia; there he had denied being "homesick." Yet here – it is the only other moment when the word comes up – he says he knows that Mr. Shimerda was "homesick." How is displacement working, then? Mr. Shimerda seems to stand in for Jim, who inverts his own journey west (thus taking himself "home") by imagining Mr. Shimerda going to Chicago, then Virginia, then Baltimore; and who sees his own homesickness as a potentially fatal disease through diagnosing Mr. Shimerda's suicide. Thus Jim tries to work through his own losses – both of his parents and of his home – by contemplating this new death. And certainly the scene in the kitchen is a scene of emotional labor, a labor that otherwise remains enigmatic.

What does that labor produce? After Mr. Shimerda's funeral, months pass before Jim sees the family – even Ántonia – again. And when he does, he is filled with hostility. Mrs. Shimerda "craftily" (78) tries to steal information from him and then acts suspicious when Jim gives it; he notices disgustedly how she places her cooked food into a quilt; Ántonia looks more and more mannish ("[she] ate so noisily now, like a man" [81]) or peasant-like ("One sees that draught-horse neck among the peasant women in all old countries" [79]); and Ambrosch's belligerence with the harness produces a "feud" between them. It is difficult not to seek a connection between these changes and Jim's preoccupation with the death of Mr. Shimerda. But what might that connection be?

Jim uses a startling locution when he describes how much Ántonia has grown. "She had come to us a child," he says, "and now she was a tall, strong young girl" (79). "Come to us"? Jim is forgetting that he arrived with Ántonia on the same train; he is identifying himself with his grandparents, who are natives in relation to all these new immigrants. Natives yet still traditional Southerners, his grandparents offer Jim continuity with his past in ways that he neither acknowledges nor recognizes. Yet Jim's hostility to the Shimerdas after Mr. Shimerda's death can be explained in terms of all-too-familiar Southern values: class superiority and related gender expectations. There is a suggestion of racism as well in Jim's insistence on Ántonia's "brown" skin and the surviving Shimerdas' links with animals (her mother "gobbles" her food, the two women "claw" the air).

Jim's identification with his family's Southern ways can be traced as well in his feelings about gifts. Even at the very outset of his relationship with Ántonia, Jim is disturbed by her offer of a ring in exchange for his help with translation. Later, he says that he worries about people who are too free in giving things away. Yet he also resists the Shimerdas' desire to take. He sees Mrs. Shimerda's request for information as crafty; he feels his grandmother is far too soft in giving away their iron pot when Mrs. Shimerda asks for it; and the feud results from disagreements about ownership and exchange.

Jim has come from a culture in which class difference is worked out through paternalistic exchanges. In such exchanges, the superior person, at his or her discretion, gives goods or services; the inferior waits until the superior is moved to give, and then gives gratitude and loyalty – docility, amiability, and happiness – in return. Thus the power differential is maintained. The Shimerdas are breaking the rules; they offer their own goods (the ring, the socks), ask for what they want (the pot, the information), and resist the superiority of the Burdens. (Ambrosch's destruction of the harness can be compared to Snopes's destruction of the carpet in Faulkner's "Barn Burning.") In short, they are contesting the ideology of paternalism. Jim's grandfather, on the other hand, exemplifies paternalism. He is indifferent to the feud, refusing to acknowledge the Shimerdas' challenges and maintaining his paternalistic relation with them; whereas his wife fears Ántonia will lose her "nice ways" in the field, he is happy with her, saying "she will help some fellow get ahead in the world" (81); and he has the foresight to see how growing corn will contribute to a world economy.

It is important, thus, to notice in what ways Jim's grandparents remain Virginians. In Virginia, the "foreigners" with brown skin are of course African Americans – within memory, slaves; in the South, cotton had shaped a world economy and at the same time solidified the power of paternalism. In their Nebraska Southern household, the grandfather is lord and master. The grandmother is likewise a familiar southern figure, a lady who talks in her "polite Virginia way" (49). Later she says, in fine female paternalistic form, just as she might describe slaves or "white trash" back home: "I will say, Jake, some of our brothers and sisters [the Shimerdas] are hard to keep. Where's a body to begin, with these people? They're wanting in everything, and most of all in horse-sense" (52).

Let us look again now at the meanings of Mr. Shimerda for Jim. What does Mr. Shimerda miss about his old country? Marrying "beneath" himself out of honor, yielding to his wife's insistence upon moving to America, he has lost a life of music, books, scholarly and priestly friends, and work as an artisan, making tapestries. Though he is clearly not of the nobility, neither is he fitted for a life of agricultural labor or for the planning required to "move up" in a mobile society. The European culture he comes from, despite its difference, is one that Jim associates with Virginia. When Jim sees Mr. Shimerda's hair, and when he sees Pavel and Peter, he is reminded of portraits on the walls in Virginia. He observes carefully Mr. Shimerda's pride in the details of his appearance; his scarf and pin are in place even in death. Mr. Shimerda's violin, and the sense of culture it represents, are foreign to the practical prairie but familiar to Virginia. Even his apparent incompetence with money is coded in America as Southern, alien to the Puritan tradition. Mrs. Shimerda enacts a rigid class hierarchy, with its attendant gestures, when she kisses Jim's grandfather's hand. Despite his embarrassment, the gesture is appropriate for the Virginia paternalism Jim's grandfather has just exhibited by giving her the cow he had meant to sell. That Mr. Shimerda would not have done what his wife did is another sign of his awareness of his class superiority, an awareness that cannot be sustained in the conditions he finds on the prairie. When Mr. Shimerda mourns his old country, then, it is in many ways not so very alien to Jim's own past. He serves for Jim as the Nebraska farm women served for Cather: as a link to the past. In this case, however, it is a weak link, offering Jim a connection with the past only at the cost of life itself.

Jim's displacing his own melancholia onto Mr. Shimerda suggests that he sees homesickness as fatal and so refuses to face his losses and grieve his Virginia past after Mr. Shimerda's death. Yet since he sees his own childhood in Ántonia, we need to look at Ántonia's response to the loss of her father and her old country as well. For clearly where Mr. Shimerda offers a failed mourning process, unsuccessful finally in giving up the lost object and forming a new life, Ántonia offers an example of successful mourning. Her emotions, unlike Jim's, are visible and tied directly to her loss. She tells stories of her old country; she remembers the paths through the woods, and talks about them; she remembers and values the culture her father has lost. But Ántonia, unlike Jim, finds a way to give up her nostalgic hopes for a repetition of the old life, and to seek out the possibilities of the new. If she emerges by the end of the novel as the more satisfied adult of the two, it is because she, unlike Jim, has worked through her losses and invented a place for herself in the new world.

Indeed, although Jim shows great empathy for Mr. Shimerda's loss of his own country, he has never been as compassionate toward himself. He has never written about, or spoken to anyone about, his unhappiness at leaving his own homeland; nor has he told readers about, or shown to other characters, any "vivid pictures" of his own past. He substitutes for his own vivid pictures, whatever they may be, the stories he has heard about Mr. Shimerda, almost breaking the boundaries of identity (["Jim's imaginings] might have *been* [my emphasis] Mr. Shimerda's memories"). Jim never becomes aware of his acts of projection and displacement and identification. Instead, Jim will identify the "figures of [his] old life" as Lena Lingard and the other hired girls, not the people he knew in Virginia, and construct a "home pasture" out of Black Hawk as Cather did with Red Cloud. Like Cather, he will use the West and Ántonia to cover his older and earlier life. Unlike Cather, Jim never returns to Virginia. Instead, he permanently displaces Dixie onto the landscape of Nebraska.

Why then does Jim not follow Ántonia's path? Perhaps it is because her sense of her past represents a less Southern sensibility than does her father's. Yet perhaps his inability to follow Ántonia's model has more to do with gender. Ántonia is a girl, Mr. Shimerda is a man. She is able to find a place within the gendered West as her father is not. And Mr. Shimerda's struggles with manhood closely resemble the struggles of Southern white men – indeed, of Cather's own father.

The narrative Jim tells in *My Ántonia* is in significant part a displaced story of Southern gender troubles. Unable to confront his Southern past directly, Jim is unable to address its impossible gender conundrums, especially those it presented for white men – heroism linked with violence and domination.

Recall Jim's responses to Pavel's deathbed story of throwing a friend and his bride to the wolves. "At night," Jim says after

hearing the story, "before I went to sleep, I often found myself
in a sledge drawn by three horses, dashing through a country
that looked something like Nebraska and something like Virginia" (41). As he did with Mr. Shimerda's spirit, here Jim offers
a glimpse into the working of his interiority – and again we have
a rare reference to Virginia. Yet we can determine neither the
landscape – Virginia? Nebraska? – nor the role Jim plays in this
fantasy. Is he the groom, or the bride, about to be forced out to
die? Is he Pavel, about to push them out? or Paul, driving the
sledge? This indeterminacy suggests the conflict Jim so rarely
expresses. On the one hand, he has, like the bride and groom,
been thrown to the wolves, to die at least to his old life. On the
other, he has tossed that old life violently out of his mind in
Nebraska, refusing to deal with it except from a great distance,
by displacement, and to a great extent unconsciously. The story
"gave us a painful and peculiar pleasure," he writes. No doubt
that masochistic/sadistic pleasure is associated with the intensity
of the feelings that must undergird such a conflict, feelings of
power and helplessness, guilt, fear and rage.

But that ambivalent pleasure also has to do with Jim's ambivalence about gender. Cather's own relation to white Southern
masculinity shifted from an early idealization of the Civil War
hero, dying in battle, to a transformation of that figure in her last
novel into the sexually predatory white man whose potential
victim is a woman, and whose weapon is his penis. *My Ántonia*
seems preoccupied with the intersections, and the conflicts, between these two violent masculinities, the one heroic and the
other simply cruel.

Jim Burden seems preoccupied with the question of male heroism. He first associates it with late afternoon sunlight and with
"heroes who died young and glorious" like Cather's "namesake"
William Boak. But instantly undercutting this romantic idea, we
see on very same page a "figure moving on the edge of the
upland . . . walking slowly, dragging his feet along as if he had
no purpose": it is papa Shimerda, neither young, glorious, heroic, nor dead. The next scene examining heroism takes us behind the scenes to show us the hero being constructed as such.
The effect is to de-romanticize the figure again. After Jim kills

the snake, Ántonia's "exultation was contagious." Not coinci-
dentally, the "great land had never looked to me [Jim] so big
and free . . ." and "I began to feel proud of [the snake], to have
a kind of respect for his age and size" (32). Yet just as the figure
of Mr. Shimerda implicitly unraveled the association between
the afternoon sun and the hero, Jim deconstructs his own heroism in killing the snake: "in reality it was a mock adventure . . .
I had been adequately armed by Russian Peter; the snake was
old and lazy, and I had Ántonia beside me to appreciate and
admire. Nevertheless, for Ántonia, I had killed a big snake – I
was now a big fellow." Although his first reaction to the events
had been petulant and blaming, when Ántonia worships him "I
began to think that I had longed for this opportunity, and had
hailed it with joy" (32). His very memory of the event is being
shaped by her interpretation.

Cather goes beyond exposing the fictionality of masculine heroism and the complicity of women in that fiction. She has Jim –
oddly – react to the snake with instant and deep repugnance that
will surface later in the novel in his description of the sensual
black man Blind d'Arnault. Elsewhere in the novel images of
objects that penetrate (by force or otherwise) are similarly coded
as dangerous and harmful, while to be penetrated elicits an
equally strong sense of disgust. Recall Jim's horror at the rape he
nearly suffers while impersonating Ántonia in Wick Cutter's
house; and recall the "dread" of going to bed discussed earlier.

The intensity of Jim's repulsion stems, I contend, from resistance to a Southern acculturation that associates violent penetration with masculinity. Jim's identifications are so frequently with
the feminine position because he cannot consciously accept an
identity as the perpetrator of sexual – and more insidiously, social – domination. The power issues that surround the bodily
representation of manhood in the South make it impossible for
Jim finally to accept the embodied masculine gender. Tempted
by its phallic power, he can never truly enjoy the perquisites of
manhood. Thus he remains undecided, ambivalent, unable to
accept or reject a masculine identity.

Let us take this hypothesis into a reading of the famous
"plough" scene. Early in the scene – just before Jim swims na-

ked, in a pleasurable merging with nature – he seems to feel nature "lift itself up to me and to come very close." This erotic (and nonpenetrative) embrace is followed by the entry of the "girls," uncannily echoing the scene of d'Arnault's embrace of the piano in Black Hawk followed by the entry of the "hired girls." But this time the girls don't "dance"; they talk about the meaning of cultural transition for their mothers and about how they will make up for male failure by living their own lives (152–3).

As if in response to their focus on female power and male insufficiency, Jim tells a story of imperial conquest, a very male story of heroism and desire, of Coronado's search for Seven Golden Cities, and of Jim's own discovery of a metal stirrup and a sword. After presenting this masculine discourse to the enthralled group, the next "gold" Jim describes is the shimmer on the river, then the "gold-washed sky" (156), and finally the famous plough, "heroic in size, a picture writing on the sun." In this context, the plough is clearly another big blade entering the earth. Gold here, as a sign of coin, may be linked not only to the golden cities but to the corn that Jim's grandfather foresees as the economic meaning of the Middle West: "It took a clear, meditative eye like my grandfather's to foresee that [the cornfields] would enlarge and multiply until they would be, not the Shimerdas' cornfields, or Mr. Bushy's, but the world's cornfields; that their yield would be one of the great economic facts . . . which underlie all the activities of men, in peace and war" (88).

Then the "forgotten plough [sinks] back to its own *littleness* [my emphasis]" (156) and the dreams of heroic masculinity wilt. Jim again is troubled by his ambivalence, the split between his own erotic feelings (which tend towards images of liquidity, merging, and nonpenetrative eroticism) and his internalized and idealized gender identity, that of the dominant Southern white man. Following this scene of diminished masculine heroism is the scene of Jim's shame, of his bloodied body, after "cross dressing" in Ántonia's bed and becoming the victim of Wick Cutter's vengeance. Jim's feelings of "disgustingness" resulting from his "disfigured face" (159) here suggest his sense of feminization, as does his blood – and his self-blame. Now occupying the woman's position, he finds both roles again "disgusting." As if to empha-size the association of penetrative manhood with ownership of slaves, Wick's anger that Jim might have gotten to Ántonia first ("so this is what she's up to when I'm away, is it") suggests he has a right to control her behavior when home and prefigures Martin Colbert's sense (in *Sapphira and the Slave Girl*) of how unbearable it would be if Henry "got there [inside Nancy] first." In this discourse, women and the landscape are there for the taking, to be ploughed, owned, and capitalized by men. It is no wonder that Jim, with his multiple identifications, rejects the traditional gendered positions – male *and* female, master *and* slave, rapist *and* victim. Unfortunately he is unable to imagine or discover a new discursive space to occupy.

Cather raises the stakes even higher when she has Jim make an explicit connection between ploughing and writing. While he is thinking of Virgil's *Georgics* (the source of the quintessentially Southern genre, the pastoral), he imagines a scene "where the pen was fitted to the matter as the plough is to the furrow." Recall his words on first seeing the land: "The new country lay open before me" (11); presumably he can write on it, then, as he chooses. It is no accident then that, a few pages later, "it came over me, . . . the relation between girls like those and the poetry of Virgil" (173). The missing connection, the unnamed "rela-tion," joins plough, pen, and penis, country, page, and woman. Writing would seem to require a willingness to occupy one side of the gender binary – that is, the penetrative.

Yet at this time Jim has moved into a "new world." His de-scription of that entry is eerily reminiscent of his entry into Ne-braska at the age of ten: "When one first enters that world [of ideas] everything else fades for a time; and all that went before is as if it had not been." Gaston Cleric's successful termination of Jim's relationship with Lena Lingard erases that past along with the woman who signifies it and constructs a homosocial, homo-erotic world that excludes women. If Jim is now writing instead of being written upon, as we saw in the early pages of the novel, the metaphoric implications are contained by heterosexual absti-nence. Such implications are further complicated by Jim's con-tinuing identifications with the "other," with the woman and the black, the objects of penetration. At the same time that he sees himself (as a Southern white man) superior to them, Jim is drawn to an identity with precisely those women who – by class or vaguely implied race – are the most marginal. Note, for example, that Ántonia is a servant even on the prairie – she works for the Burdens – before she moves to work for the Harlings. As we saw, she is racially inscribed as well, with her brown eyes and skin and curly "wild-looking" brown hair (17).

How can we read the outcome of Jim's continuing conflict with white Southern masculinity? If we judge by the clues from his later life, the prognosis for growth is poor. When he goes home in the summer from Harvard, he finds the plough doing its same old work, the "old pasture land . . . being broken up into wheatfields and cornfields." He finds this agricultural domination "beautiful and harmonious," like watching the "growth of a great man or of a great idea"; in the context of the novel, both of these "growths" are notably masculine (197). When he remembers his dream of Lena, the reaping hook is missing; she no longer has, in his imagination, any phallic capacity to do damage or enact power. His job has come from family connections, his Southern mother's. He works as a lawyer – neither a scholar like Gaston Cleric, excavating the past, nor a farmer and parent like Ántonia, whose penetrated fruit cave gives birth to the future. He lives in New York, his marriage is cold and distant; and his desires now seem regressive, for all he wants is to go back and be a boy again, to be re-mothered by Ántonia, to find a first family.

These clues suggest that his life and his identity have taken form in very traditional ways, in languages that he has known from his earliest life. If his resistance to phallic power and his identification with the position of "other" had been resolved more fruitfully, perhaps he would have found a new language for himself, one whose power lay not in the inherited binaries of violation and violated, but in an erotics of equal relation, mutuality, and dialogue.

Instead, Jim's life reinscribes, rather than moving beyond, the invisible traces of his Virginia childhood. The final words of the novel suggest the perpetuation of this structuring absence. At the conclusion Jim feels again "that obliterating strangeness" of his first night on the prairie. But now, he says, "I had the sense of coming home to myself." For "this [the Nebraska path] had been the road of Destiny . . . which predetermined for us all that we can ever be." It is startling to notice again the full denial of his first and most determining past, his Virginia childhood. Indeed, it would not be until Cather went home to Virginia herself that she would become capable of remembering – and writing, openly – the painful conflicts of her own Southern past, in *Sapphira and the Slave Girl.*

Willa Cather, I think, was finally drawn to write about the South not only to recuperate directly her earliest identity but also to address issues of power, particularly gender concerns. For her, the South, its dialect, its landscape, its hierarchical social arrangements, and its related gender system, represented the contradictions of the world first known. The safety and security the traditional South had offered, if only in myth and retrospect, dovetailed for Cather with the safety and security of her experience of her first home. Yet the inequalities and injustices of that South, and the resentment of them reflected in calling herself a "dang'ous nigger," dovetailed with her love for freedom and the new. Her forced, sudden, and total departure from the South thus produced and represented for her a complex nexus of the trauma of loss, of ambivalence toward the lost object, of the processes of grieving, and of the possibilities of the new.

Cather was to tell this story of traumatic removal repeatedly, in various guises. The last version appears in *Sapphira and the Slave Girl,* where Nancy Till the slave girl stands in for Willa Cather; Montreal, to which she escapes, for Nebraska; and Nancy's return to the Mill House for Cather's fictional and factual return to her first and hence most ineradicable home, Willow Shade. In *My Ántonia* she told the story of Southern loss not only through Jim but through the Shimerdas, especially Ántonia and her father, and through the other "hired girls" who "had . . . been awakened and made observant by coming at a tender age from an old country to a new" (127). Figuring herself as several characters, Cather traces out alternative processes of cultural and personal grief. Figuring herself as Jim in particular, she shows the lingering effects of repressing the ineradicable past.

Like Jim, too, Cather struggled with the costs and benefits of Southern gender arrangements, knotted together so inseparably with race and class. As a young writer, she sought in her own cultural past some example – whether that of heroic Confederate soldier or feminized gentleman – of successful deviance, from the competitive model of American manhood dominant at the time. Later in her life, after reconciling gender and vocation through her relationship with Sarah Orne Jewett in stories like "Old Mrs. Harris" and in *Sapphira*, she explored the contradictions and complexities of Southern womanhood(s), seeking in her own cultural past a femininity that offered more power and possibilities, and more openness to racial difference, than white Northern womanhood. Southern constructions of gender, in short, initially seemed to offer Cather useful alternatives to American womanhood as well as manhood.

Cather wrote *My Ántonia* during the middle period of her struggles with gender and region, with masculine and feminine, with Virginia and Nebraska. *My Ántonia* is thus a novel that, while it openly embraces Nebraska and Ántonia, keeps a closet date with Virginia and Southern white manhood. The buried text of *My Ántonia* is the story of the burden of Jim's, and Cather's, Southern history, of how to relieve – and how to be broken by – that burden.

Just as Jim writes his memories of Mr. Shimerda's ghost in his manuscript, Cather sought directly to summon, face, and bury the ghosts of her own Southern past in *My Ántonia*. Like Jim, she also sought to replace Virginia with another, truer home in the West. Both located the meanings of their childhoods in Ántonia, though neither had met an "Ántonia" until well past early childhood. The novel (including the framing materials) thus became a way of representing while evading Cather's own relation to the past. Like Jim's stifled grief, Cather's process of mourning in writing *My Ántonia* was incomplete. Only later in life did she directly confront her memories of the South, especially but not exclusively in *Sapphira and the Slave Girl*. Sadly, Jim Burden apparently never does. His inability to mourn means that he will remain emotionally paralyzed and permanently immature, never becoming an adult. Yet given the gender options offered by his cultures, whether Southern or Western, this limbo may not have been a bad place to reside. At least Jim avoided the oppressive forms of manhood he encountered in the South and, in different forms, in the West.

NOTES

1. Quoted in Mildred Bennett, *The World of Willa Cather* (Lincoln: University of Nebraska Press [rev. ed.], 1961), p. 200.

2. For the full text of Cather's poem "The Namesake," see *April Twilights*, ed. Bernice Slote (Lincoln: University of Nebraska Press, 1976), p. 26.

3. See, for example, Katrina Irving, "Displacing Homosexuality: The Use of Ethnicity in Willa Cather's *My Ántonia*," *Modern Fiction Studies* 36 (Spring 1990): 91–102, and Judith Fetterley, *My Ántonia*, Jim Burden, and the Dilemma of the Lesbian Writer," in *Gender Studies: New Directions in Feminist Criticism*, ed. Judith Spector (Bowling Green, Ohio: Bowling Green State University Popular Press, 1986), pp. 43–59.

4. Sandra Gilbert and Susan Gubar, *The Madwoman in the Attic: The Woman Writer and the Nineteenth-Century Literary Imagination* (New Haven: Yale University Press, 1979).

5. W. E. B. DuBois, *The Souls of Black Folk* (New York: Penguin, 1989).

6. Edith Lewis quoted in Sharon O'Brien, *Willa Cather: The Emerging Voice* (New York: Oxford, 1987), p. 43. I have drawn heavily on O'Brien's understanding of Cather's struggles with gender.

7. Willa Cather, *Willa Cather on Writing: Critical Studies on Writing as an Art* (New York: Knopf, 1949), n.p.

8. Bernice Slote, ed., *The Kingdom of Art: Willa Cather's First Principles and Critical Statements 1893–1896* (Lincoln: University of Nebraska Press, 1966), p. 448.

9. James Woodress, *Willa Cather: A Literary Life* (Lincoln: University of Nebraska Press, 1987), p. 31.

10. Willa Cather, *My Ántonia* (Boston: Houghton Mifflin, 1918), p. 8. Citations in the text are to this edition.

11. Slote, ed., *Kingdom of Art*, p. 112.

12. My thanks to Noel Polk for this observation.

13. Richard H. Millington, "Willa Cather and 'The Storyteller': Hostility to the Novel in *My Ántonia*," *American Literature* 66 (December 1994): 689. My thanks to David Leverenz for calling my attention to this essay's usefulness in decoding Cather's South.
14. Ibid., p. 692.
15. Ibid., pp. 712–13.
16. Susan Rosowski, "Willa Cather and the Fatality of Place: *O Pioneers!, My Ántonia,* and *A Lost Lady*," in William E. Mallory and Paul Simpson-Housley, eds., *Geography and Literature: A Meeting of the Disciplines* (Syracuse: Syracuse University Press, 1987), p. 81.

5

"It Ain't My Prairie": Gender, Power, and Narrative in *My Ántonia*

MARILEE LINDEMANN

FOR years I avoided working on Cather's *My Ántonia* because I was distracted and annoyed by the insipidness of its narrator, Jim Burden. The novel Cather claimed as her favorite struck me as either a failed experiment in point of view or a successful but not always interesting exploration of the mind of a man incapable of understanding women. Rethinking the novel recently, however, I have embraced a more positive version of the latter view, as Jim's failures have come to seem spectacular and endlessly fascinating, the critical point of the novel and not a sign of its flaws. My reassessment has been shaped as much by political events and the cultural climate of the 1990s as by the provocative body of feminist critical study of *My Ántonia* that has developed in the past twenty years. Indeed, Jim Burden now strikes me as the narrative equivalent of the Senate Judiciary Committee listening in the fall of 1991 to Professor Anita Hill's testimony about Supreme Court nominee Clarence Thomas, an event that has resonated throughout the political culture of the U.S. for much of the decade. On Capitol Hill, a woman speaks, but the all-male committee's power to interpret and pass judgment upon her speaking is, at least in the short run, of much greater consequence. For the senators, those interpretations are determined by a range of competing and often peculiar demands, including political expediency, the ideological pressures created by race and gender differences, and even the sexual histories of individual senators. Individually and collectively, the committee members shape, reshape, and misshape "their" Anita Hills – as a professionally ambitious backstabber, a psychologically unbalanced sexual fantasist, a politically motivated perjurer, or a well-intentioned martyr whose allegations of sexual harassment (largely because of the committee's own bungling) came too late and under circumstances too bizarre to change the outcome of the confirmation process. Thus, in the movement from testimony to judgment to media melodrama, the speaking woman is less subject than object, at once a construction of male powers and desires, the screen upon which they are projected, and the field within which they are interpreted.[1]

The distance between Jim Burden and committee chairman Joe Biden (and, at certain mean-spirited points in his narrative, between Jim Burden and the prosecutorial Arlen Specter) does not to me seem great, and the resemblances between "his" Ántonia and the Judiciary Committee's Anita Hill(s) have helped rekindle my interest in Cather's novel by suggesting that Jim's narrative is as racked by ideological pressures and discursive uncertainties as the transcripts of the Senate hearings. After all, Jim is, like most of the senators, a lawyer, and he presents his "account" of Ántonia to the unnamed speaker in the Introduction – whom I will, following Jean Schwind, designate "Cather"[2] – in a "legal portfolio."[3] He is also, like them, beset by conflicts and contradictions: endowed with a romantic disposition that seems at odds with the cool logic of the lawyer; passionate about the prairie country of his youth but stuck for the most part in New York; in love not with his handsome wife but with his memory of a Bohemian girl. Finally, as "Cather" makes clear, Ántonia functions for Jim much as Anita Hill functioned for the inept yet powerful senators – that is, not as an autonomous subject but as a symbol or screen. In his narrative she serves not as a "character" in the novelistic, psychologically complex sense but as a "central figure" who "mean[s]" for Jim (and for "Cather") "the country, the conditions, the whole adventure of our childhood" (Intro). Her purpose is neither to speak nor to act but merely to "mean." "I had lost sight of her altogether," remarks "Cather," "but Jim had found her again after long years" (Intro). Ántonia is a symbol to be decoded, an object to be "lost," "found," named, and claimed: "My Ántonia." Jim's claiming of Ántonia is both rhetorical and ideological, and it poses a range of challenges to feminist readers of the novel. In what follows I will explore the significance of his claim, both to the text he narrates and to the career of Willa Cather.

Feminist criticism has in an important sense reinvented Cather in recent years, contributing significantly to reversing the decanonization of the Pulitzer Prize–winning novelist that occurred during the 1930s and 1940s.[4] Her contemporary recanonization is largely the result of feminism creating an entirely new context for reading Cather and thus a new climate of reception for her works. Though all feminists may share an interest in gender issues, the variety of critical techniques and theories they deploy – psychoanalytic, new historical, archetypal, and women's cultural – has established Cather as a major American writer with important links to other women writers and a significant place in several literary traditions. Judith Fetterley and Marjorie Pryse, for example, see Cather as the culmination of "regionalism," a mode of writing practiced chiefly by women in the nineteenth century and characterized by empathic narration and female protagonists who become capable of adult identity by venturing into female communities and becoming aware of their connections to other women.[5] Elizabeth Ammons places her at the center of a diverse group of women writers who, at the turn of the century, constituted a "pioneer generation" determined to "invade the territory of high art" that historically had been the province of men and united in their preoccupations with the institutionalized oppression of women and ethnic minorities, the figure of the female artist, and "the need to find union and reunion with the world of one's mother."[6] Cather is accorded a prominent place in several feminist studies that focus on the plots and symbols that recur throughout fiction by American women, including the story of housekeeping or domestic ritual, the myth of Demeter and Persephone, and the use of space and landscape as structuring devices.[7]

Most importantly, perhaps, the emphasis on gender has raised compelling questions about the writer's sexual and literary identities, questions that have haunted studies of *My Ántonia* at least since 1971, when Blanche Gelfant identified Jim's recurring dream of Lena Lingard coming to kiss him with a curved reaping-hook in her hand as the locus of his and Cather's fears of sexu-

ality.[8] In 1987, however, by making a cogent, unapologetic case
for Cather's lesbianism, Sharon O'Brien's feminist psychobiogra-
phy *Willa Cather: The Emerging Voice* opened up a vast interpretive
territory, as critics immediately began combing the novels and
short stories for signs of how sexuality is translated into textual-
ity, how lesbianism is masked or disguised to evade detection and
censure.[9] In the case of *My Ántonia*, the foregrounding of issues
of desire and sexuality has drawn attention to the puzzling relationship between Jim and Ántonia and to the unstable gender
identities of the novel's two main characters. Critics have contended that Jim is an autobiographical mask for the confusing
attractions Cather felt toward the pioneer women of her own
Nebraska youth, or that both characters are homosexuals whose
friendship is built out of their mutual experience of sexual deviance.[10]

Problematic as some of these readings may be, the value of
such energetic revisionism is that it begins to situate Cather more
clearly within modern – and Modernist – contexts of sexual mal-
aise and locates in her art signs of that resistance to gender-role
socialization so apparent in the writer's own life. But critical preoccupations with questions of character and point of view – with
ascertaining whether Jim Burden is a "real" man or a cross-
dressed authorial surrogate – have skewed debate about *My Ántonia* in significant ways. Feminist readers are likely to be annoyed by Jim's fastidiousness and applaud Ántonia's subversive
and stubborn vitality – when, for example, she asserts at the age
of fifteen, "I can work like mans now" (123) – while Jim is
horrified by the power and sexual ambiguity of her presence and
annoyed by everything from her suntan to her table manners.

The difficulty with such reactions – and I count my own early
impatience with Jim among them – is that they psychologize
issues of gender, power, and desire, while *My Ántonia* goes much
further, wrestling determinedly with the challenge of narrativiz-
ing and historicizing those same issues. Consider, for instance,
the terms most frequently used by critics to describe the treatment of desire in *My Ántonia*. They are all at bottom psychological: "invalidation," "evasion," "displacement," "concealment,"
"oscillation," and "renunciation."[11] Such a focus is limited in a

number of respects. It localizes desire (and the whole complex of issues associated with it) in particular characters, symbols, or situations; it confuses to a greater or lesser degree life (Cather) and art (Jim); and it flattens a text that works strenuously against naive notions of representation into a series of portraits or case studies – of, depending on the critic's point of view, the struggling homosexual, the lonely lesbian, the ''strange'' bisexual,[12] the unhappy heterosexual.

Late in her career, Cather herself sharply attacked the psychologizing tendencies of literary interpretation, complaining bitterly that a generation of readers ''violently inoculated with Freud'' would find little to appreciate in the work of her predecessor Sarah Orne Jewett.[13] Cather's skepticism about psychoanalysis (and her disturbing xenophobia and antisemitism) aside, the remark serves to remind us that the Introduction to *My Ántonia* establishes Ántonia not as a character but a ''figure.'' A fictional ''character'' is not, of course, a real person, though much of our pleasure in reading novels derives from the belief that well-rounded ''characters'' are ''like'' us, that they choose and suffer and triumph much as we do.

A ''figure,'' however, is several steps further removed from ''reality'' than a ''character'' and so is psychologically less substantial, complicating the reader's desire to ascribe motives, affix labels (''lesbian,'' ''bisexual,'' ''heterosexual''), or establish sympathetic connections. A figure is by definition an abstraction – an image, an outline, an illustration or drawing, like the eight line drawings by W. T. Benda that illustrate *My Ántonia*. Finally, though, as I suggested earlier, a figure may also be rhetorical – that is, a figure of speech. This last possibility is carefully foregrounded in the Introduction to *My Ántonia*, as ''Cather'' twice calls attention to the fact that Ántonia is a figure made of words. She emerges first in the ''talk'' ''Cather'' and Jim engage in while crossing Iowa together on a train, and then in Jim's ''writing down'' his memories of her (an act that in part precedes their ''talk'' chronologically but is revealed later in narrative time). Made of words, Ántonia generates words as readily as she generates children, for their ''talk'' in the observation car ''kept returning to [her],'' and Jim writes about her in an urgent manner that belies his assertion that he did so only to "amuse [him]self" on his cross-country trips. His appearance at "Cather's" apartment on a "stormy winter afternoon" months after their meeting on the train and his apparent desire to be quickly rid of "the thing about Ántonia" suggest that Jim is anxious to escape the proliferative logic of the process he initiated: figures begetting figures in so quick and slippery a fashion that he cannot "take time to arrange" them and doubts they have "any form."

That Ántonia is described only as "a central figure" and not "*the* central figure" in "Cather" and Jim's "talk" is crucial to realizing how deeply preoccupied *My Ántonia* is with the logic, the process, and the power of figure-making. The indefinite article forces us to extend that logic, to acknowledge, for example, that Ántonia is at least a figure of a figure: Jim figures her, but "Cather" figures Jim – while somewhere off in the distance Cather figures "Cather" as a writer, in the 1918 Introduction, who could not write the story of Ántonia.[14] As the layers multiply, that "central figure" grows increasingly insubstantial, and the questions for feminist readers of *My Ántonia* grow increasingly complex. One of the most complex questions, however, may be stated succinctly: What does it mean that the novel Cather identified not only as her best but as a real contribution to American letters[15] is the story of a woman ("Cather") figuring a man (Jim Burden) figuring a woman (Ántonia)? By attending to this question, we might arrive at a deeper understanding of how the novel, in foregrounding the problem of how women perceive and are perceived in masculinist culture, broods upon and elucidates profoundly feminist issues, though its author almost certainly did not intend to create a self-consciously "feminist" work.

Indeed, throughout her long, shrewdly managed career as a writer, Cather publicly denied that gender was psychologically powerful or culturally meaningful. As a young magazine columnist in the 1890s, for example, she boasted to readers of the Pittsburgh *Home Monthly* that "the fact that I was a girl never damaged my ambitions to be a pope or an emperor," and she urged parents in selecting books for their children to avoid making the "hateful distinction" between "boys' books" and "girls' books" for as long as possible, noting that she preferred "the books that are for both."[16] She ridiculed feminists and other women writers so habitually that critics have recently wondered if the concept of "female misogyny" might not apply to her.[17] "Hateful" to her or not, however, the distinction between "boys' books" and "girls' books" – and a host of other gender-based distinctions – was made in the culture Cather lived and wrote in, and she was more troubled by it than the bravado of her early pronouncements suggests. For Cather, the figure-making process that is scrutinized in *My Ántonia* was embedded in the same cultural system that worked systematically, though in her case unsuccessfully, to undermine a girl's "ambitions to be a pope or an emperor"; so the process is also a contest – a struggle not just to make figures but to assign them meanings as well. By these terms, desire is the longing for interpretive power and cultural authority, and gender is the basis upon which the sides are drawn. And the figure of a woman figuring a man figuring a woman is the site where the two sides meet.

At first glance the imbricated narrative structure of *My Ántonia* would seem to tilt the scales in favor of the women's side in the battle for linguistic power waged in the novel. If "Cather" figures Jim, then "she" gets the first and last word and is thus the authoritative speaker. Many revisionary readings of the novel have hinged upon this kind of reasoning, noting that Jim's credibility as a narrator is severely undermined in the Introduction and systematically questioned throughout the text. Jim's "romantic disposition" and his imperialistic rhetorical gestures – "*My Ántonia*" – mark his perceptions as distorted, subjective, and partial, and open up the text to allow every reader to construct alternative Ántonias. We do so with help from the critical female voices that periodically erupt out of Jim's narrative: Ántonia pointing out to Jim that education is a luxury privileged "little boys" like him can afford, while for her working "like mans" is a grim economic necessity (123); Lena Lingard laughing at his views on marriage and disparaging "family life" as "all being under somebody's thumb" (291–2); Frances Harling echoing "Cather's" description of Jim as "romantic" in his tendency to "put a kind of glamour over" the hired girls and asserting the authority of her own perceptions: "I expect I know the country girls better than you do" (229).

These dissenting views, coupled with the evidence of "Cather's" editorial work on Jim's narrative – the footnote on the pronunciation of Ántonia's name and the insertion of the Benda sketches[18] – de-authorize Jim's version of the story and guide the reader toward the "real" – accurate, authoritative – story. What these arguments overlook, however, is that the contest enacted in *My Ántonia*, much like the Hill-Thomas imbroglio, has almost nothing to do with accuracy or credibility. If that were the case, the obvious debunking of Jim's vision in the Introduction would be a glaring flaw in the narrative. If Jim's credibility is primarily what is at stake, then the Introduction offers a dead giveaway – tantamount to a mystery writer revealing "who done it" on the second page. If Jim were merely a "romantic," then hard-nosed readers like me could dismiss him as insipid and curl up instead with Cather's unmediated portraits of powerful women, *O Pioneers!* and *The Song of the Lark*. Rather than credibility, though, power is what is at stake in *My Ántonia*, and from that standpoint the women's side in the novel may be found as powerless as the group of female legislators who stormed Capitol Hill to protest the Judiciary Committee's handling of Professor Hill's allegations.

Right or wrong, accurate or inaccurate, credible or incredible, the women's voices in *My Ántonia* suffer from a crisis of location that dangerously diminishes their ability to construct a counter-story to the romanticized "boys' book" that is Jim's *Ántonia*. Relegated at every point to the margins of the text, these voices are so muted that they seem to be echoes of echoes, and their power to qualify or correct Jim's perceptions is dubious at best. He may not be "right," but no alternative view is ever loudly or clearly articulated. The only woman who speaks directly – in her own voice rather than in the mediated voices presented in the main narrative – is "Cather," and her speaking is confined to the supplementary textual space of the Introduction, though her role as editor is fitfully apparent beyond that space. Moreover, "Cather" is such an elusive figure that she is barely present in her own brief narrative, receding away from the reader as she swerves continually away from herself and toward Jim, her conversation with him, and their shared experience of growing up "in a little prairie town,"

buried in wheat and corn, under stimulating extremes of climate: burning summers when the world lies green and billowy beneath a brilliant sky, when one is fairly stifled in vegetation, in the colour and smell of strong weeds and heavy harvests; blustery winters with little snow, when the whole country is stripped bare and grey as sheet iron. (Intro)

"Buried," "stifled," and "stripped bare" aptly describes the condition of women's voices in *My Ántonia*; and Cather's revisions to the Introduction for the 1926 edition indicate more clearly that "Cather" suffers as fully from this condition as the women whose voices are selectively recalled and transcribed by Jim Burden. The later Introduction significantly scales back the figure of "Cather," obscuring in particular her status as a writer and excising the only explicit reference in the text to her editing of Jim's manuscript – the cryptic remark that "the following narrative is Jim's manuscript, *substantially* as he brought it to me" (1918, xiv, emphasis added). Cather's occlusion of "Cather's" active role in shaping the manuscript suggests that her purpose in revising the Introduction was more than merely aesthetic.

That occlusion profoundly destabilizes *My Ántonia* by making uncertain the connection between the Introduction and Jim's narrative, and by making the few editorial marks upon his narrative seem in a sense to have come from nowhere. The charge of a "romantic disposition" may compromise Jim's credibility and establish an ironic distance between "Cather's" (and Cather's) and Jim's perceptions, but by 1926 "Cather" had been "stripped bare" of the power or authority necessary to challenge the larger claim Jim makes to Ántonia. Unwilling or unable to offer a glimpse of "her" Ántonia, "Cather" stands as a sign of Cather's deep skepticism about women's ability to compete in the contest to figure themselves in a culturally powerful way.

Beyond the Introduction, the stifling of women's voices figures prominently in both the plot and the structure of Jim's narrative. Like most first-person narrators, Jim shows signs of being in love with the sound of his own voice and is fully in control of all the other voices in the text, for his power to record events, impressions, and other people is uncontested. Even as a boy, Jim revels in the "considerable extension of power and authority" he experiences when he realizes he is alone in his grandparents' house for the first time during the tumult occasioned by Mr. Shimerda's suicide – an experience he recalls as "delightful" and "pleasant" despite the sorrowful event that made it possible (100). As "alone" in his narrative as he is in his grandparents' house, Jim's linguistic "power and authority" extend to a preoccupation with the sounds of women's voices and the content of their speech – from the useless chatter of a grandmother who "always talked, dear woman: to herself or to the Lord, if there was no one else to listen" (111) to the "conventional expressions" and "small-town proprieties" that became "very funny, very engaging, when they were uttered in Lena's soft voice, with her caressing intonation and arch naivete" (281). In both cases, Jim cannot detach women's speaking from his culture's genderbound assumptions about female behavior: He hears his grandmother's talk to herself through the filter of bourgeois, late-Victorian associations of women with gossip and religion, while Lena Lingard's "soft voice," endowed with the physical power to "caress" and the suspicious but appealing quality of "arch"-ness, reaffirms her connection in Jim's mind to dangerous, uncontrolled sexuality. Again, what women say matters less than how they are heard, and Jim's power to situate women's words in such charged social, spiritual, and erotic contexts assures that he is the primary maker of meaning in *My Ántonia*.

Jim functions in the text as a sexual-linguistic gatekeeper and translator, for when women speak in his narrative they do so in quotation marks, and that is perhaps the clearest sign of the deep-seated gender trouble being examined in the novel. Women may seem at times to speak for themselves and actively to resist the meanings Jim would impose upon their stories, but even the most resistant, subversive voices are already his, not theirs. Their speech is always marked, framed, claimed, and circumscribed, and theirs are the muted voices of alien others contained within a larger voice – unmarked because it is the illusion of absolute presence, power, and authority.

Perhaps the best example of the limits imposed upon female linguistic power in Jim's narrative is Frances Harling, whose critique of Jim's romanticism has already been mentioned. Socially, Frances is at least Jim's equal, if not slightly his better, since her family is already well settled in Black Hawk and prospering in business when Jim's grandparents begin the transition from farm to town life. She is also a ''grown-up'' when he is still a boy, acknowledged as ''a very important person in our world'' whose ''unusual business ability'' earned her ''a good salary'' as her father's chief clerk (148–9). More importantly, though, Frances is credited with an unusual verbal dexterity, a capacity for speaking and comprehending a variety of what might be called genderlects. She is able on the one hand to talk with her father ''about grain-cars and cattle, like two men,'' to arrange deals, and to collaborate with Jim's grandfather ''to rescue some unfortunate farmer from the clutches of Wick Cutter, the Black Hawk money-lender.''

But while Frances drives out into the country ''on business,'' she also performs the women's work of paying visits, going ''miles out of her way to call on some of the old people'' and deftly switching into another sociolinguistic mode: ''She was quick at understanding the grandmothers who spoke no English, and the most reticent and distrustful of them would tell her their story without realizing they were doing so'' (150–1). Frances, too, is a figure of speech, and her speech is a powerful mixture of male and female, town and country, New World and Old World. Since she is not, like Jim, inclined to ''take sides'' (229), Frances's easy movement across rhetorics and social categories marks her as a figure of generosity and reconciliation, but her power is ultimately cross-checked in his narrative. She may assert superior knowledge of the country girls he views through a veil of glamour, but the assertion stands isolated and unsupported in Jim's telling of the story. Her counter-story is, like ''Cather's,'' hinted at but never effectively told. Framed by memory and choked by quotation marks, Jim's Frances offers no details of her alternative view of the class of women Jim claims as his personal possession: ''my country girls'' (201). Frances knows them, but Jim owns them. The novel seems haunted by the possibility that real power is the power to possess – a house, a person, a voice, a narrative – and that women are decidedly lacking in that power.

For Jim, the language of imaginative possession and the self-aggrandizing rhetorical gesture are part of his birthright as a native-born American male endowed with a "romantic disposition." To Jim, language reflects the sexual order of the universe, so he resents Ántonia's occasionally taking "a superior tone" with him because "I was a boy and she was a girl" (43). Jim's sense of language as a manly means of claiming the world suggests that his romanticism is inherited from Emerson, who exalted the poet as "true land-lord! sea-lord! air-lord!"[19] Like his forebear's poetry, Jim's narrative represses or circumvents the possibility that a woman might aspire to be "land-[lady]! sea-[lady]! air-[lady]!" Indeed, the immigrant daughters who captivate Jim's attention are doubly estranged from the vocabulary of possession that is so comfortable to him because it is marked not only as manly but also as "American." "Foreigners" like Ántonia and Lena must struggle even more acutely than Frances Harling with a language that is not theirs in ways that go beyond Jim's proprietary quotation marks. Their speech is restricted to discourses of dispossession that stand in sharp contrast to the confident "my"-ness of Jim's voice, and he functions as a kind of linguistic policeman, monitoring women's voices and citing them for their failure to speak appropriately.

Ántonia is on more than one occasion criticized for using language deemed inappropriate to her gender. Jim notes disapprovingly that she "could talk of nothing but the prices of things, or how much she could lift and endure" (126) and attacks her for "jabber[ing] Bohunk" when the two confront a rattlesnake in prairie-dog town (46). Jim's harsh judgments of Ántonia in these situations contrast with the respect he accords Frances Harling for her ability to talk with her father "like two men" and to understand the grandmothers "who spoke no English," indicating that for the immigrant woman language is a field mined with much greater risks. Ethnic difference compounds and complicates the difficulties created by gender difference, making Ántonia doubly vulnerable and doubly burdened. Just as he polices her appearance for signs of masculinization in her youth and diminishment in middle age, Jim polices Ántonia's speech for evidence of gender or ethnic transgressions, both of which, in his judgment, she commits: She talks "like mans" and "jabber[s] Bohunk."

Of all the women figured in Jim's narrative, Lena Lingard emerges as the most serious challenge to his authority because her voice, even in his eroticized transcription of it, is so powerful and so completely at odds with his adolescent fascination with her body that it nearly shatters the frame he constructs for it: *nearly*. Jim lingers to the point of fetishizing over the details of Lena's physicality – the "miraculous whiteness of her skin" (165), "the swelling lines of her figure" (167), her sleepy, violet eyes and "slow, undulating walk" (201) – and seems uninterested in or bewildered by the radical difference between his image of her and Lena's sense of herself. Lena's consuming professional ambition fails to register with Jim, though she announces it in her first appearance in his narrative when she visits Ántonia at the Harlings after moving into town to study dressmaking with Mrs. Thomas (161). Thus, after she visits him in Lincoln with news that she is already established in business for herself and they rekindle their friendship, Jim confesses to being "puzzled" by her success and seems skeptical about it: "Her clients said that Lena 'had style,' and overlooked her habitual inaccuracies" (279). Jim cannot bring himself to concur in the judgment that Lena has "style," because style is a sign of independence and creativity, so he distances himself from the judgment by attributing it to "clients" and undercuts it by suggesting those clients don't pay careful attention to Lena's work.

In the section of his narrative that bears her name, Jim constructs Lena not as an artist whose "style" might be worthy of praise but as a muse who should inspire creativity in (male) others: "If there were no girls like [Lena and the other country girls] in the world, there would be no poetry" (270). When she fails in that role by distracting Jim instead of inspiring him – "I was drifting," he laments, "Lena had broken my serious mood" (288) – Lena essentially disappears from Jim's narrative; he takes off to Harvard with Gaston Cleric and then settles into his loveless, childless marriage. Later, Jim reports that Lena became "the leading dressmaker of Lincoln" (298) before conquering San Francisco with Tiny Soderball (301–2). She appears once more twenty years later to encourage Jim to go see Ántonia, still unmarried and closely connected to Tiny, with a dress shop in an apartment building around the corner from Tiny's house. In their presence, the once gushing boy is a suddenly laconic man, remarking only, "It interested me, after so many years, to see the two women together" (328). Finally, though, when Ántonia shows him a photograph of Lena, Jim reverts to his habit of judging and adoring the dressmaker piece by piece, confirming that she looks "exactly like" the picture, "a comely woman, a trifle too plump, in a hat a trifle too large, but with the old lazy eyes, and the old dimpled ingenuousness still lurking at the corners of her mouth" (350).

Jim's Lena is a Scandinavian Marilyn Monroe, a figure of excess ("too plump," "too large") who cannot be contained and therefore must be abandoned (by leaving Lincoln, by dropping her out of the story). However, his efforts to reduce Lena to an object, the static sum of her bodily parts, are stymied by her resilience, her social and economic mobility, and a degree of "self-possession" that causes him to "wonder" (279). Lena's "self-possession" makes her a point of friction in Jim's narrative, because it is a sign of how remote and disengaged she is from the spectacle Jim and other men make of her body. That disengagement is evident in her indifference to gossip, her hostility to marriage, and her clear-eyed sense that desire is chiefly a game whose rules she understands well enough to exploit. "Old men are like that," she tells Jim when he expresses concern about the attentions paid her by Ordinsky, the Polish violin teacher who lives across the hall from her. "It makes them feel important to think they're in love with somebody" (290). Abundant yet self-possessed, Lena is a figure of excess un*con*tainable and un*ob*tainable. She is literally and figuratively too much, yet not enough, for Jim, for something is always withheld, left over for herself. Enigma and siren, she must be forcibly abandoned, and she is. "My Lincoln chapter closed abruptly," Jim announces in the paragraph that concludes Lena's section of his narrative. The statement is fraught with the tension her figure arouses in him and betrays his need to assert control over it: "My" insists that the story is his (not hers), "Lincoln" defines it as the story of a city (not a woman), "chapter" calls attention to its literariness and its small size, and "closed abruptly" imbues the action of ending the story with significant physical force.

Despite the psychological "self-possession" that even Jim can't help noticing, Lena's speech is, like Ántonia's, confined largely to a rhetoric of dispossession that signals her place in the novel's interrogation of women's power and powerlessness. She articulates an awareness of her dispossession bluntly yet clearly in the story of Ole Benson's scandalous obsession with her, an episode Jim recalls in "The Hired Girls." Benson is the farmer plagued by misfortune whose wife, "Crazy Mary," escapes from the asylum in Lincoln and takes to chasing Lena around with a corn-knife because her discouraged husband abandons his cornfield on summer afternoons to help the Norwegian girl watch her cattle. During one of these escapades Lena's cattle are scattered, and she asks Jim and Ántonia to help her get them back together. Mrs. Shimerda, who watches the scene from a window and "enjoyed the situation keenly," suggests Lena is to blame in the incident, prompting a reply whose rhetoric is significant:

"Maybe you lose a steer and learn not to make somethings with your eyes at married men," Mrs. Shimerda told her hectoringly.

Lena only smiled her sleepy smile. "I never made anything to him with my eyes. I can't help it if he hangs around, and I can't order him off. It ain't my prairie." (169)

Later, Lena will offer a more expansive and positive explanation of her relationship with Ole, telling Jim that "There was never any harm in [him]" and that his companionship provided relief from the tedium of being "off with cattle all the time" (282). At this early juncture, however, her speaking is a series of denials and negations, a statement of what she has not done, cannot do, and most importantly perhaps, does not own. She voices a far-reaching sense of dispossession that is at once linguistic, sexual, economic, legal, and territorial. Young, immigrant, and female, Lena is aware that she lacks the "power and authority" Jim discovers when he is left, like the child protagonist of the popular film, "home alone." Her assertion that "It ain't my prairie" exploits and critiques American expressive traditions that forge symbolic links between women's bodies and frontier landscapes, for the prairie that is not hers is the scene of a struggle provoked by a body that is not fully hers either – since everyone in the community feels entitled to watch it, judge it, long for it, and threaten it. (Even in church, "the congregation stared at" it [167], and Crazy Mary offers to "trim some of that shape off" Lena with her corn-knife [168].) Limited to a discourse of negatives – "never," "can't," "ain't" – and unable to say "my" of the prairie she farms or the body she inhabits, Lena articulates the dilemma of the woman who understands and even exploits the rules of the game but realizes she is powerless to change them.

Because it is such a loaded psychosexual symbol, the prairie is arguably the primary site of contestation in *My Ántonia*'s analysis of gender in/and the figure-making process, so Lena's declaration that it "ain't [hers]" takes on special significance. For her, the association of women's bodies with the land is grotesquely literalized as an odor that clings stubbornly to her: "After I began to herd and milk, I could never get the smell of the cattle off me" (292). And her family's little house on the prairie is a space of negative abundance and oppressiveness, particularly for women: "[Lena] remembered home as a place where there were always too many children, a cross man and work piling up around a sick woman" (291). Lena succeeds in turning over the body/land metaphor and exposing its problematic underside, but the dispossession she experiences on the prairie prompts her flight away from home and through a succession of ever larger towns and cities – Black Hawk, Lincoln, San Francisco. She deconstructs the metaphor but has nothing to install in its place, and so retreats from the field of battle. She has a counter-story but lacks a language adequate for telling it. Eventually, as we have seen, she all but disappears from Jim's narrative, leaving him both the prairie and the last word.

Ántonia, on the other hand, returns to the prairie from Black Hawk, insisting to Jim, "I belong on a farm. I'm never lonesome here like I used to be in town" (343). Far from critiquing the body/land metaphor, Ántonia seems to endorse it wholeheartedly. Her rejection of town life leads to a happy entanglement in nature that includes working the land, raising a huge brood of children, and even being kind to animals. Explaining her fear of guns to Jim, Ántonia says, "Ever since I've had children, I don't like to kill anything. It makes me kind of faint to wring an old goose's neck" (342). Instead of talking "like mans," as she had in her rebellious youth, in the last section of the narrative Ántonia talks like a mother, suggesting that for her the prairie is a space of (limited) power because she ultimately acquiesces to the sexual and symbolic order Jim had enunciated and attempted to enforce in their childhood, because "I was a boy and she was a girl" (43). Where Lena resists Jim's ordering and interpreting, Ántonia aids and abets it, holding forth so readily on domestic management, the quirks of her children, and her early concern for the trees in her orchard ("They were on my mind like children" [340]) that Jim's assertion that she could "make you feel the goodness of planting and tending and harvesting at last" (353) seems justified.

In contrast to Lena's overwhelming erotic energies, Ántonia's maternal power is no threat to Jim's masculine discursive power. Images of Ántonia endure in his mind and his narrative with the safe stasis of symbols. She represents to him "immemorial human attitudes which we recognize as universal and true" and is immortalized as the mother of sons who "stood tall and straight" (353). She and her husband may own part of the prairie, but linguistically Ántonia is no more able to claim it than is Lena. Indeed, "I belong on a farm" suggests that in some sense the prairie owns her, while symbolically she clearly remains Jim's possession. Through her, Jim is able to achieve a "sense of coming home to [him]self," to lay claim to "the precious, the incommunicable past" (371–2).

* * * * *

To many, this reading of the novel will no doubt seem to have demonized Jim Burden and perversely turned Cather's elegy of pioneer life into a paranoid feminist allegory on the evils of male authority. My aim has not been to demonstrate that Jim is a bad guy or a cruel character or any sort of "character" at all. My goal has been to suggest that Cather's manipulations of narrative form and voice in *My Ántonia* indicate that she remained ambivalent about female artistic and cultural power well beyond the period of creative emergence so capably explored by Sharon O'Brien. Moreover, Cather saw a sexual imbalance of power operating on the deepest levels of the text and shaping the conditions of its interpretation, a preoccupation that informed her work throughout the 1920s, as she continued to grapple with the form of the novel and with the sexual dynamics of American literary history. The muted state of women's voices in *My Ántonia* is refigured, for example, in the silent agony of Mother Eve, the Indian mummy discovered in *The Professor's House* with her mouth frozen open "as if she were screaming," and in the roar of the underground river that so disturbs Jean-Marie Latour in the "Stone Lips" sequence of *Death Comes for the Archbishop*.[20]

Sensing the increasing masculinism of American literary culture and critical discourse, Cather sought, particularly in her preface to *The Best Stories of Sarah Orne Jewett*, to formulate a model of creativity rooted in the womanly "gift of sympathy"[21]; but she seems always to have doubted that "sympathy" was a weapon of sufficient power in the battle between "boys' books" and "girls' books" that grew so heated in America after World War I. Published in 1918 and revised in 1926, when the cultural effects of the war were clearer and more settled, *My Ántonia* marks a crucial point in her long, uneasy examination of gender's determinative impact upon a range of social powers because in the main body of its narrative there is no space that is not-Jim. His control of the first-person pronoun and his ability to place female subjectivity in quotation marks make his power pervasive if not unchallenged. In the process of analyzing a man's power to "figure" a woman, Cather figures Jim as the god of his narrative – creator and sovereign of the world he calls into being from the opening, "I first heard of Ántonia on what seemed to me an interminable journey across the great midland plain of North America" (3).

The Widow Steavens may briefly take over as narrator in "The Pioneer Woman's Story" and even echo Jim's rhetorical claim to possessing "my Ántonia" (313), but her telling is framed by Jim's quotation marks and her story is offered chiefly to lay the groundwork for his apotheosis of Ántonia as Earth Mother. She performs the necessary task of restoring Ántonia's dignity in Jim's eyes (following the birth of her first child out of wedlock) and pronouncing her fit for the symbolic role he will ultimately confer upon her: "Ántonia is a natural-born mother" (318), Mrs. Steavens declares. Mrs. Steavens is an authoritative presence – "brown as an Indian woman, tall, and very strong," with a "massive head" that as a child reminded Jim of "a Roman senator's" (307) – but Jim controls and possesses her speech as fully as he does that of every other woman in his narrative. What she says is of less import than what he makes of her speaking.

A final example will serve to underscore how entangled *My Ántonia* is in issues of gender, power, and possession and so return this discussion to the questions of laws and lawyers with which it began. One of the more puzzling highlights of Jim's final visit to Ántonia is the story of the murder-suicide that ends the unhappy marriage of Wick Cutter and his "giantess" wife (211), a tale related "in great detail" and to the delight of everyone by Ántonia's eldest son, Rudolph (361). At the heart of the "perpetual warfare" (210) of the Cutter marriage is, significantly, a dispute about property, for Black Hawk's shiftless money-lender is "tormented" (361) by the prospect of his wife's outliving him and "shar[ing] his property with her 'people,' whom he detested" (213). When a state law is passed guaranteeing "the surviving wife a third of her husband's estate under all conditions" (361), Cutter is so determined to circumvent his wife's right to inherit that he murders her, shoots himself, and then summons witnesses to prove that he has outlived her.

In this bizarre episode, the new law is on the woman's side, but the literal and symbolic weapons possessed by the man – the gun Cutter uses to carry out his plan and the letter he leaves offering a legal explanation for his actions ("any will she might secretly have made would be invalid, as he survived her" [363]) – prove to be vastly more powerful. So impressed by the story is

Jim that he admits that "Every lawyer learns over and over how strong a motive hate can be, but in my collection of legal anecdotes I had nothing to match this one" (363–4). Cutter's letter turns his crime into both a story and a legal maneuver, conjoining the discourses of law and narrative as effectively as Jim does in describing himself as a collector of "legal anecdotes." With his dying breath, Cutter explains to neighbors that the killing of his wife was simply a matter of putting his "affairs . . . in order" (363), suggesting that his fastidiousness goes somewhat beyond Jim's, though the murderer and the narrator share a similar predilection for monitoring and attempting to control female behavior.

Published two years before women gained the right to vote, *My Ántonia* thus allegorizes the extreme precariousness of women's claims to power and property and seems pessimistic about the possibility of legal change leading to the more far-reaching social and cultural changes necessary to make women's voices authoritative. A dead woman is, after all, silent; and in the layered telling of *My Ántonia* the voice of even a living woman is barely audible. On Cather's prairie as on Capitol Hill, a woman speaks, but men retain the power to transcribe, interpret, and render judgment upon her words. The novel's feminism resides, then, not in its several portraits of indomitable pioneer women but in its bleak and unflinching examination of the limitations placed upon such women, for in analyzing the power struggle at the heart of language as an ideological system, Cather figures a man who figures a woman with her mouth effectively shut.

NOTES

1. The Hill-Thomas fiasco has spawned a veritable industry of analysis and interpretation from a wide range of perspectives. For a sampling of these analyses, see Toni Morrison, ed., *Race-ing Justice, En-Gendering Power: Essays on Anita Hill, Clarence Thomas, and the Social Construction of Reality* (New York: Pantheon Books, 1992) and Robert Chrisman and Robert L. Allen, eds., *Court of Appeal: The Black Community Speaks Out on the Racial and Sexual Politics of Clarence Thomas vs. Anita Hill* (New York: Ballantine Books, 1992). Paul

Simon, a Democratic senator from Illinois and member of the Judiciary Committee, brings an insider's perspective and a sense of history to his analysis in *Advice & Consent: Clarence Thomas, Robert Bork and the Intriguing History of the Supreme Court Nomination Battles* (Washington: National Press Books, 1992), while Timothy M. Phelps and Helen Winternitz write as political journalists in *Capitol Games: Clarence Thomas, Anita Hill, and the Story of a Supreme Court Nomination* (New York: Hyperion, 1992).

The contest over the public meaning of the Hill-Thomas hearings obviously continued long after Thomas was confirmed to the court, and Hill and her supporters may claim a victory of sorts in the results of the 1992 elections: The president who nominated Thomas was himself defeated, and record numbers of women were elected to public office in what the media deemed "the year of the woman" in American politics. It might also be argued that the vilification of First Lady Hillary Rodham Clinton can be partly ascribed to what I would call the Anita Hill effect – i.e., a backlash against women who appear too "aggressive" in their claims to public, discursive power. What concerns me here, however, is the imbalance of rhetorical power between Professor Hill and the Senators that mattered so much in the short run.

2. Jean Schwind, "The Benda Illustrations to *My Ántonia*: Cather's 'Silent' Supplement to Jim Burden's Narrative," *PMLA* 100 (January 1985): 51–67. I use this designation chiefly for the sake of convenience and retain the quotation marks to distinguish Cather the person from "Cather" the persona. I should also note that Schwind's essay is rich with insights on many matters other than the illustrations to the novel and that her discussion of the differences between the introductions to the 1918 and 1926 editions helped stimulate my thinking on many of the issues considered here.

3. Willa Cather, *My Ántonia* (1918, rev. 1926; Boston: Houghton Mifflin, 1954), Introduction (n. pag.). Future references to this edition will be made parenthetically by page number; references to the unpaginated introduction will be followed by the abbreviation Intro; references to the 1918 edition of the novel will be preceded by 1918.

4. For an analysis of this process, see Sharon O'Brien, "Becoming Noncanonical: The Case against Willa Cather," in Cathy Davidson, ed., *Reading in America* (Baltimore: Johns Hopkins University Press, 1989), 240–258.

5. See Judith Fetterley and Marjorie Pryse, eds., "Introduction," *American Women Regionalists, 1850–1910* (New York: W. W. Norton, 1992), xi–xx.

6. Elizabeth Ammons, *Conflicting Stories: American Women Writers at the Turn into the Twentieth Century* (New York: Oxford University Press, 1992), 5.

7. The studies alluded to here are Ann Romines, *The Home Plot: Women, Writing, and Domestic Ritual* (Amherst: University of Massachusetts Press, 1992); Josephine Donovan, *After the Fall: The Demeter-Persephone Myth in Wharton, Cather, and Glasgow* (University Park: Pennsylvania State University Press, 1989); and Judith Fryer, *Felicitous Space: The Imaginative Structures of Edith Wharton and Willa Cather* (Chapel Hill: University of North Carolina Press, 1986).

8. Blanche Gelfant, "The Forgotten Reaping-Hook: Sex in *My Ántonia*," in *Women Writing in America* (1971; Hanover, NH: University Press of New England, 1984), 94–116.

9. Sharon O'Brien, *Willa Cather: The Emerging Voice* (New York: Oxford University Press, 1987). O'Brien's influence has been widely felt in recent criticism on Cather, creating a wave of readings attentive to feminist and psychosexual issues. See, for example, Judith Fetterley, "*My Ántonia*, Jim Burden, and the Dilemma of the Lesbian Writer," in Karla Jay and Joanne Glasgow, eds., *Lesbian Texts and Contexts: Radical Revisions* (New York: New York University Press, 1990), 145–163; Katrina Irving, "Displacing Homosexuality: The Use of Ethnicity in Willa Cather's *My Ántonia*," *Modern Fiction Studies* 36 (Spring 1990): 91–102; Claude J. Summers, " 'A Losing Game in the End': Aestheticism and Homosexuality in Cather's 'Paul's Case,' " *Modern Fiction Studies* 36 (Spring 1990): 103–119; Eve Kosofsky Sedgwick, "Across Gender, Across Sexuality: Willa Cather and Others," *South Atlantic Quarterly* 88 (1989): 53–72; and Sandra Gilbert and Susan Gubar, *Sexchanges*, vol. 2 of *No Man's Land: The Place of the Woman Writer in the Twentieth Century* (New Haven: Yale University Press, 1989), esp. 169–212. For additional lesbian and gay readings, see note 10.

10. The first position – i.e., that Jim is Cather "speaking in masquerade" of her love for women – is implicit in Joanna Russ's "To Write 'Like a Woman': Transformations of Identity in the Work of Willa Cather," in Monika Kehoe, ed., *Historical, Literary, and Erotic Aspects of Lesbianism* (New York: Harrington Park Press, 1986), 77–87. Russ argues that all of Cather's male personae seem flawed or inconsistent and that heterosexual relationships seem impossible

in her fiction because they camouflage the story of "the lesbian in love with the heterosexual woman because she believes there is nobody else to be in love with" (84). Though provocative, Russ's argument is undermined by its reliance on dubious speculations about "real male experiences" (85) and the consequences of Cather's supposed lack of involvement in an openly lesbian community. The second position – i.e., that Jim and Ántonia are homosexual friends – is developed in Timothy Dow Adams's "My Gay Antonia: The Politics of Willa Cather's Lesbianism," in Kehoe, 89–98. Dismissing the characters' major life choices as "marriages of convenience that serve as masks for their sexual variance" (97), Adams grounds his (also provocative) reading of the novel on contemporary notions of homosexual and lesbian identity that seem remote from the world of *My Ántonia*. Since, for example, Jim and Ántonia never discuss yet seem to "understand each other's sexual preferences" (97), one must suppose that they are equipped with "gaydar," the mechanism/intuition that supposedly enables homosexuals and lesbians to detect the presence of kindred spirits in unlikely places and situations – or so we insist when we happen to judge correctly.

11. Gelfant argues that Cather "consistently invalidates sex" for many of her characters (95) and that *My Ántonia* is shaped by "a pattern of sexual aversion" (99). Such terms as "evasion," "displacement," and "concealment" are key to arguments that Cather seeks to mask her lesbian desires in *My Ántonia*; see, for example, Fetterley and Irving. O'Brien uses the term "oscillation" in "Gender, Sexuality, and Point of View: Teaching *My Ántonia* from a Feminist Perspective," in Susan J. Rosowski, ed., *Approaches to Teaching Cather's "My Ántonia"* (New York: Modern Language Association, 1989), 140–145. "Renunciation" is central to Gilbert and Gubar's discussion of Cather's treatment of desire, as they argue that her "greatest literary problem . . . resulted from her fatal attraction to a renunciation of passion" (205).

12. Gelfant uses this label to describe Ántonia (107).

13. Cather's "Miss Jewett," in *Not Under Forty* (New York: Knopf, 1936), 76–95, is an expanded version of the preface she wrote for the two-volume collection of Jewett's stories she edited for Houghton Mifflin in 1925. The later essay is remarkable for its pessimism on matters that go far beyond Freud – a sign, perhaps, of how embattled Cather had come to feel in the intervening decade. In the first version, for example, she happily anticipates the pleasure

with which "the young student of American literature in far distant years to come will take up this book and say, 'A masterpiece!' as proudly as if he himself had made it." See Cather, Preface to *The Best Stories of Sarah Orne Jewett* (Boston: Houghton Mifflin, 1925), 1:xix. By 1936, the "young student" is reconceived as "perhaps of foreign descent: German, Jewish, Scandinavian," an "adopted American . . . cut off from an instinctive understanding of 'the old moral harmonies' " (*Not Under Forty*, 93–4) and thus uninterested in Jewett (and, one must suppose, Cather).

14. The ending to the 1918 Introduction differs substantially from that of 1926, for in the earlier edition the following conversation occurs after Jim has written "My Ántonia" across his portfolio:

    "Read it as soon as you can," he said, rising, "but don't let it influence your own story."

    My own story was never written, but the following narrative is Jim's manuscript, substantially as he brought it to me. (xiv)

    In the version of 1926, the only sign that "Cather" is a writer is the desk at which Jim sits to put a title on his manuscript.

15. Cather is reported to have offered this assessment of the novel in 1938 on the twentieth anniversary of its publication. See Mildred Bennett, *The World of Willa Cather* (1951; Lincoln: University of Nebraska Press, 1961), 203.

16. Cather's early work in journalism has been collected and reprinted in William M. Curtin, ed., *The World and the Parish: Willa Cather's Articles and Reviews, 1893–1902*, 2 vols. (Lincoln: University of Nebraska Press, 1970). For the two columns referred to here, see 1: 368, 337.

17. Gilbert and Gubar, 174.

18. This is the essence of the argument made by Schwind. Though I agree that the function of the introduction and the illustrations is to undercut Jim's credibility as a narrator, I see these textual supplements as too unstable and problematic to enable us, as Schwind suggests, "to read Cather's story [by reading] 'Cather's' story" (55). In an analysis published after I had written this essay, Judith Butler argues a point similar to Schwind's from a different, more psychoanalytic direction. Arguing that the transfer of authority from the introductory narrator to Jim is a false one, Butler suggests that this act of feminine dissimulation "facilitates the claim to the text that she only appears to give away" and that such false transfers are a recurring movement within Cather's texts, "a figure for the crossing of identification which both enables and conceals the

workings of desire." See " 'Dangerous Crossing': Willa Cather's Masculine Names" in *Bodies that Matter: On the Discursive Limits of "Sex"* (New York and London: Routledge, 1993), 143–66, esp. 145–53.

19. Ralph Waldo Emerson, "The Poet," in Stephen E. Whicher, ed., *Selections from Ralph Waldo Emerson* (Boston: Houghton Mifflin, 1957), 241.
20. Willa Cather, *The Professor's House* (1925; New York: Vintage, 1973), 214; Cather, *Death Comes for the Archbishop* (1927; New York: Vintage, 1971), 125–36.
21. Cather, Preface to *The Best Stories of Sarah Orne Jewett*, 1:xii.

Notes on Contributors

Elizabeth Ammons is Harriet H. Fay Professor of Literature at Tufts University. She is the author of *Conflicting Stories: American Women Writers at the Turn into the Twentieth Century* (1991) and *Edith Wharton's Argument with America* (1980). She is also the editor of a number of volumes, including *Short Fiction by Black Women, 1900–1920* (1991) and, with coeditors, *Tricksterism in Turn-of-the-Century American Literature: A Multicultural Perspective* (1994) and *American Local Color Writing, 1890–1920* (1998).

Anne Goodwyn Jones is Professor of English at the University of Florida. She is the author of *Tomorrow Is Another Day: The Woman Writer in the South, 1859–1936* (1981), *Dead Lovers Are Faithful Lovers* (1994), and *Haunted Bodies: Gender and Southern Texts* (1998).

Marilee Lindemann is Associate Professor of English at the University of Maryland. She is the author of *Willa Cather: Queering America* (1998) and the editor of Cather's *Alexander's Bridge* and *O Pioneers!* for Oxford University Press.

Sharon O'Brien is John Hope Caldwell Professor of American Cultures at Dickinson College. She is the author of *Willa Cather: The Emerging Voice* (1987) and *Willa Cather* (1994). She is also the editor of the three-volume Library of America edition of Willa Cather's writings as well as of several editions of Cather's novels.

Miles Orvell is Professor of English and American Studies at Temple University and the author of *Flannery O'Connor: An Introduction* (1972; rpt. 1991), *The Real Thing: Imitation and Authenticity in American Culture, 1880–1940* (1989), and *After the Machine: Visual Arts and the Erasing of Cultural Boundaries* (1995).

Selected Bibliography

Bennett, Mildred. *The World of Willa Cather.* Lincoln: University of Nebraska Press, 1961.

Bloom, Harold, ed. *Willa Cather's My Ántonia.* New York: Chelsea House, 1987.

Fetterley, Judith. "*My Ántonia,* Jim Burden, and the Dilemma of the Lesbian Writer," in *Lesbian Texts and Contexts,* ed. Karla Jay and Joanne Glasgow. New York: New York University Press, pp. 145–163.

Fischer, Mike. "Pastoralism and Its Discontents: WIlla Cather and the Burden of Imperialism," *Mosaic* 23 (Winter 1990): 31–44.

Fryer, Judith. *Felicitous Space: The Imaginative Structures of Edith Wharton and Willa Cather.* Chapel Hill: University of North Carolina Press, 1986.

Gelfant, Blanche H. "The Forgotten Reaping-Hook: Sex in *My Ántonia,*" *American Literature* 43 (1971): 60–82.

Irving, Katrina, "Displacing Homosexuality: The Use of Ethnicity in Willa Cather's *My Ántonia,*" *Modern Fiction Studies* 36 (Spring 1990): 91–102.

Lambert, Deborah. "The Defeat of a Hero: Autonomy and Sexuality in *My Ántonia,*" *American Literature* 43 (1971): 76–90.

Lewis, Edith. *Willa Cather Living.* New York: Alfred A. Knopf, 1953.

Martin, Terence, "The Drama of Memory in *My Ántonia,*" *PMLA* 84 (1969): 304–11.

Miller, James E., Jr. "*My Ántonia*: A Frontier Drama of Time," *American Quarterly* 10 (1958): 476–84.

Millington, Richard H. "Willa Cather and 'The Storyteller': Hostility to the Novel in *My Ántonia,*" *American Literature* 66 (December 1994): 689–718.

Murphy, John J., ed., *Critical Essays on Willa Cather.* Boston: G. K. Hall, 1984.

Murphy, John J. *My Ántonia: The Road Home*. Boston: G. K. Hall, 1989.

O'Brien, Sharon. "Becoming Noncanonical: The Case Against Willa Cather," in *Reading in America: Literature and Social History*, ed. Cathy N. Davidson. Baltimore: Johns Hopkins University Press, 1989, pp. 240–58.

O'Brien, Sharon. " 'The Thing Not Named': Willa Cather as a Lesbian Writer," *Signs: Journal of Women in Culture and Society* 9 (1984): 576–99.

O'Brien, Sharon. *Willa Cather*. New York: Chelsea House, 1994.

O'Brien, Sharon. *Willa Cather: The Emerging Voice*. New York: Oxford, 1987.

Rosowski, Susan. *The Voyage Perilous: Willa Cather's Romanticism*. Lincoln: University of Nebraska Press, 1986.

Rosowski, Susan, ed. *Approaches to Teaching Cather's My Ántonia*. New York: Modern Language Association, 1989.

Schroeter, James, ed. *Willa Cather and Her Critics*. Ithaca: Cornell University Press, 1967.

Schwind, Jean. "The Benda Illustrations to *My Ántonia*," *PMLA* 100 (January 1985): 51–67.

Sergeant, Elizabeth Shepley. *Willa Cather: A Memoir*. Lincoln: University of Nebraska Press, 1963.

Stouck, David. *Willa Cather's Imagination*. Lincoln: University of Nebraska Press, 1975.

Woodress, James. *Willa Cather: A Literary Life*. Lincoln: University of Nebraska Press, 1987.

Duets

Cynthia Atkins
&
Alexis Rhone Fancher

with photos by
Alexis Rhone Fancher

For my good friend,
Karen, with love.
Alexis Rhone
Fancher
9/18/22

Harbor Editions
Small Harbor Publishing

Duets
Copyright © 2022 CYNTHIA ATKINS and ALEXIS RHONE FANCHER

Cover art by Alexis Rhone Fancher
Cover design by James Fancher and Alexis Rhone Fancher
Book layout by Hannah Martin and Allison Blevins

DUETS
CYNTHIA ATKINS AND ALEXIS RHONE FANCHER
ISBN 978-1-7359090-8-0
Harbor Editions,
an imprint of Small Harbor Publishing

CONTENTS

Duets

FOREWORD

What a joy it was to collaborate together on *Duets*. Alexis and I met in the ethers of the internet over a decade ago. We became fast friends over our shared passion for poetry, jazz, and an obsessive affinity for Robert Altman's enigmatic film, *Three Women*. In the years since, we have read together at poetry venues in the flesh and virtually. In early 2021, we tossed around the idea of writing ekphrastic poems together, responding to different visual artists. As we became more intrigued, our thoughts turned to publishing our efforts, and we feared running into legal impediments. Alexis has taken thousands of exquisite photographs over the course of her life, and we realized we had a plethora of choices. That's how *Duets* began. The result is ten photographs and a responding poem from each of us.

Our voices and styles could not be more different. Our work has benefited from our mutual respect for our individual aesthetics, our beautiful sisterhood, and our friendship. The title, *Duets*, seemed to come naturally, as has every aspect of this collaboration—writing about family, love, loss, sex, death, pain, and healing. We hope these pages give our readers pleasure as well as room to wonder. I am so grateful to Alexis for her friendship, mentorship, collaboration, and the indelible photos that inspired these poems.

— Cynthia Atkins

"WE ARE ALL HOPPER PAINTINGS NOW"

Jonathan Jones, The Guardian, *UK (27 March 2020)*

That's me, solo table at *The Automat,* staring into a cold cup of tea; me, just out of frame, driving up to the lonely pump jockey in *Gas*. My sister says I have a "bad picker," that my type (well-hung and irresponsible) is very very bad for me, and she's right. *I wouldn't know a good guy if he snatched me up off the street in broad daylight,* I tell her. *My point, exactly,* my sister chides.

I decide not to tell her about the stranger I'm chatting with online. He wants to send me on a train trip, meet him in Detroit, all expenses paid, and I admit, the thought makes me wet. That's me, the woman reading in *Compartment C Car,* hurtling cross county toward a brand new life. I text him that I love Detroit, that I'm a fool for muscle cars. He says he's a poet and an artist and a Buddhist. That he hasn't owned a car in years.

I confess, romance never ends well for me. Sometimes the loneliness screams so loud I want to drown myself in a tawdry romance novel with a sappy ending or a bottomless glass of rye. Sometimes I want to hitch a ride with a comely vagabond, a poet from Michigan, drive off into the sunset. *I lived 15 years with a Lakota Sioux medicine man on Pine Ridge Indian reservation in SD,* he texts. *Lived on a deserted tropical island off the coast of Thailand, in a Tibetan Buddhist monastery in Kathmandu, traveled Europe, lived amongst Bedouin Arabs in the Negev desert.* I text back a smiley face and wait. *I want to hitchhike to Tierra del Fuego,* he responds. *Wanna go?*

If only he knew! I'm the woman staring out the bay window in *Cape Cod Morning,* desperate for my latest true love to reappear. He said he's going to the store for bread, gas up the Chevy. *Be right back.* The cloudy sky mirrors my mood. I wait. And wait.

You should know better, my sister says. *There are no rescuers anymore.* I know that. I'm the usherette leaning against the wall in *New York Movie*. I've seen that film a dozen times; I'm lost in reverie. Dressed in a thoughtful blue uniform, rebellion looks like the strappy-assed shoes, half-hidden on my feet.

Alexis Rhone Fancher

DIMINUTION, 11 AM

after Edward Hopper

Blue to yellow, the voice told me
not to bathe. The voice said the window
is a guardrail. Said today is just like tomorrow.
There is no safety from the noise
and the sorrow of birds. Told me to sit
very still, like a red clay pot on a shelf.
The voice said don't take out the trash,
don't make-up the bed. Beauty only makes
pain bellow worse, until the mattress takes up
all the air in the room. Said to deadbolt the door
where latchkey brats dwell. Once, my breasts
were savvy as two new bucket seats.
The railroad tracks took my love to another town,
to raise another woman's children. The voice said
the sun will crack your skin like paint on
an old wall. The voice said you're not here,
you're an erasure. Said the radio would tune out
the pathos of loose wires. Little motes
of silence trip the air, my lips are hugging
the voice. The chatter of teeth. Make yourself
naked, make yourself null. Make yourself
small as a toothpick in his teeth, with shoes like daggers.

Cynthia Atkins

SELF-QUARANTINE DAY 240

The days moved with the pace of a caged lion
— "July In The Jardin des Plantes" by Claire McAllister

It's almost like before, less the sounds.
No swish of tires on asphalt.
No children playing kickball in the street.
No love-struck teenaged Romeo, smoking blunts
sitting on the curb, endlessly texting some lucky girl.

Just the blast of hip hop from the FedEx truck
each time the deliveryman drops off a package.

My husband lopes from room to room.
I'm drinking too much coffee.
The ocean breeze makes our thin windows shake.
In California, no one double panes.
I haven't heard the tamale man in weeks.

Today our housekeeper appears at her usual time.
We who have hugged for 15 years, now hug
from across the room.
It feels wrong to both of us. I won't say it, but I'm relieved
she's left her teenaged son at home.

The barking dog's owner has been evicted.
No one to bark at anyway.
Sometimes, I miss the din.
I can't believe I wrote that.

Alexis Rhone Fancher

SOCIAL DISTANCING

My ex-brother-in-law died this week
in the middle of a Tsunami pandemic, this illness
of global might. And at this moment, when
the world is shutting down each last concert
and diner—I'm remembering that it was he
who taught me about jazz. At 15, my friends
listened to Peter Frampton, as I inhaled
Miles Davis, Stanley Turrentine, Coltrane's
long vowels. Today, the news is bleak,
and it's not too far-fetched to imagine
all of us breathing with masks on. We will not be
getting dressed for weddings or funerals
any time soon—all markers of life—be damned.
Nocturnes in the moon light where people
are singing a cappella out their windows.
Stitch by stitch, we pick up where
we left off. We now file this under
biblical or epic—Our daily rituals
parted like an ocean. Invisible venom
in the snake's jaw, now laws keep us
six feet apart, keep us from touch.
Awash in all our natures, this will be
the portent of who we really are. A new normal—
comedians without laughter, jazz without
smoky rooms, burying your ex-brother-in law
with a prayer and lethal hands.

Cynthia Atkins

IDENTITY THEFT

I'm telling you, I don't know who I am. No one else knows, either. I've lost my phone, my money, my keys, and ID. And now I can't find my boy. Maybe it's a robbery, or just a bad dream. The one where night falls early. The one where dead family shows up, Cory, the first-grade bully who'd shadow me home, and the creepy neighbor with grabby hands from when I was ten. And there's Raul, a man I had a crush on in college. And my younger sister, *deus ex machina*, who swoops to my rescue (again) and gives me a twenty, but it blows away. When I ask her for another, she shrugs, mutters something our mom used to say about *not throwing good money after bad*. The man-crush from college asks me to lunch at a dingy cafeteria, so I know it must be a dream. Raul's been missing for decades. Presumed down over the Pacific, I overheard at our reunion. At the counter, I order grilled cheese on whole wheat, my son's favorite. Hard to fuck up grilled cheese. Raul, in front of me in line, pays, I think, for both of us. But the cashier puts out his hand, says, *That'll be $5.50, please.* Then I wake up hungry. And my ID, keys, and my boy are still gone. It's one of *those* days, straw yellow light, windless. Second summer they call it, that brief, ephemeral part of October brimming with magic and hot, torpid air. Days listless as my sister recovering from a summer cold, as still as my dead boy.

Alexis Rhone Fancher

WHEN THE WELL RUNS DRY

Did the owls in tree branches know before us—
that first they would come for touch, until we no longer needed
our skin, until our bodies are tin cans, rattling down
the road in the amphitheater where all our old
selves dwell. We live in a box to avoid a virus,
we live in a virus to avoid a box. I used to be a little girl
in pigtails, practicing how to whistle in the March wind.
It blew through me and sound went inward,
screeching loud as a train pulling into a station.
I used to have neighbors, they used to throw
stones. Now we send our love through living rooms.
First they came for the candlesticks, then
our unmentionables. I want to look at someone
who looks me back. I need to feel a face after rain.
I want to wash my hands until I find the source
where loneliness hangs her hat. We are so bellicose
and tribal—we are tight-lipped as telegrams. Riled by want,
touching computer screens with groomed fingers
as flies pass to and fro. Like our last blown out birthday candles,
we are huddled and hungry as a pack of wolves on the coldest
night of the year. The subway rips through the city,
opens its doors, my face pushes through water to breathe.

Cynthia Atkins

BAD MOTHER

My boy died young.
I was a bad mother.
So was my mother.
My best excuse?
When she died young,
I fell off the earth.
Think thud/careen not spiral.
Think death wish. Free-fall.
A blueprint, the way I see it.
Soupçon for self-loathing,
with a narcotic chaser.
(Lovers who'd sell me out
for a half-gram of coke.)
Not good choices.
My mother threw me to the wolves:
loved my sister (the easier one)
and my brother more,
died when I needed her most.
My dead boy sealed my fate.
My only one.
I pondered suicide,
learned to police my head.
Mind over matter, my mother said,
but she never lost a child.
My near-fatal accident at twenty,
the day my little brother almost drowned,
even then, my mother had two spare kids.
I should have had more.

Alexis Rhone Fancher

JEWISH SINGLES

She held a pink can of TAB in her right hand,
bangles on her hairless wrist, a beehive hairdo—
her Liz Taylor look. When sad, her eyes
went small like gold purses, clicked shut.
The color kodak family of smiles
faux as a salesman's pitch. Our dad took
        all the photos, until he didn't.
One by one, mom met them at "Jewish Singles"
The *femme* perfume on her black cocktail dress
lingered until dawn. One night, my sister baby-sat,
we slimed and puckered with mom's make-up.
We gorged the rouge dark into a widow's peak.
        Eclipsed in the medicine cabinet,
        we found the little pink plastic quark of tablets—
        one for each day of the month.
I felt the ten commandments gasp for air—a goldfish
out of water in my gut. Picturing our mom
on the couch at Uncle Irv's, her legs captured by
his pasty belly. That night I bled for the first time,
        discovered the ache of women.
My new flannel pajamas, ruined. Some days,
a black dog lived on a street in my heart—
barked and jabbed at the wire fence
where God stamped a jinx on me.
        In a December blizzard,
while we ate popcorn and played hangman, our mom
drove the wicked snowy roads, as her Liz Taylor
eyelashes blinked with the flashers—that disk
of a hole to get to the tome, not made in stone—
but feathers in her other bed at Uncle Irv's.

Cynthia Atkins

24

ROADKILL, SAN PEDRO

Yesterday a black cat's severed head was found in my neighbor's driveway. Just the head. *Halloween's around the corner,* my lover says. Like that explains everything. I think it might be coyotes, but she says no, finding just the head is indicative of ritual sacrifice. *If the coyotes got 'em,* she assures me, *they'd leave more behind.* My lover is reading a book about humans as predators who invade a territory, deplete its resources, infect its inhabitants, then move on, and do it all again. She says it's science fiction. I say there's nothing fictional about it. Honestly, I don't know why we're still together. Except for the sex. How she knows exactly where to touch me. How I cannot get enough of her mouth. *If we could just stay naked,* I tell her, *we might have a shot.* The neighbor's new baby cries and cries. Today, for thirty minutes. I timed it, in case something happened and the detectives come calling. *You're a born rescuer,* my lover says. I think that means she loves me. *There's a kitten,* I tell her, *inside a drainpipe on the corner of 5th and Nelson, in front of the ILW Local 63.* When I mention I want to rescue him, name him Piper, she snaps. *Are YOU going to change the litter box?* Each day we spat over trifles. Wertmüller or Pasolini. Smooth or crunchy. Reggae or Ska. She thinks we should blow our savings, fly to Patagonia, like Chatwin. Traverse South America. I think we should write our will, choose a cemetery, spend that money on a double-wide. We aren't getting any younger. I want things settled, tidy, but she won't budge. *I hope to God I die first,* I tell her. *Leave you with all the chaos.* She laughs. *Don't be naive,* she says. *There is no God.*

Alexis Rhone Fancher

NINE UN-LIVES

Who knew air freshener could kill you?
Who knew that cherry smelly thing hanging
from a rearview mirror could be lethal—
but if you're a young black man, just coming
from changing your two year old's diaper,
just heading off to the store for more,
and maybe a candy bar, too—
if you're that young man, a boy really,
with a smile as wide as a cat's whiskers,
a smile wiped off the map
by a taser, mistaken for air-freshener,
a gun? When you were nine, called your mother,
told her not to worry, be home by dinner.
At 18, you slung a ball inside
a hoop as if a rabbit's foot of luck.
Who knew air-freshener hanging from
the mirror would be the lowest fruit?—
In this life, even God might stop you
for a faulty blinker, expired tags.
You left home 30 minutes ago, anonymous, a dad.
An hour later, your life is infamous,
a hashtag, a body bag with an air-freshener
staring at you in the mirror. A young man,
setting out to the store for some diapers,
for a toddler with braided hair.
She wakes from a nap to her
next life—no diapers, no father—Black cats
dancing on the windshields of America.

Cynthia Atkins

FRIDAY NIGHT AT THE CANDLELIGHT LOUNGE

She was better than I expected, hunched over the mic, arms and legs entwined with the silver stand like she was fucking it. My ex-lover Pete said she sang jazz ballads mostly, throaty and low. *Almost like Billie*, he said, how she lagged behind the beat, her voice catching on the blue notes. Pete said I should catch her act, if I was in town. Look, it was June in L.A.—the gloom fogged my vision. Pete warned me. *Careful! She's bad news. Lonely. Clingy.* But those days I was needy, too. I didn't care that her nose was crooked, her speaking voice little more than a whisper. I overlooked her slouch and her wandering eye, those clothes she wore, wrinkled Dockers and a food-stained shirt. After her set, she stood in the doorway. Her untamed black hair, a frizzy halo. Her hands in her pockets. Her eyes on me. She made my fingers ache. I got up from my ringside table, left my jacket on the chair. *You want a drink?* I asked her. When I returned from the bar with two tequila shooters, she was sitting in my chair, wearing my jacket. A noticeable improvement to her outfit. We clinked glasses. *Salud!* Pete said she was a cheap drunk. *Two rounds after each set,* he laughed, *she turns into a slut on wheels.* Already her head sagged against my shoulder. She had a tiny snore I found endearing. *Whatever you do, don't take her home,* Pete warned. Of course, he'd say that. He had what they call "graveyard love" that "I don't want you anymore but I don't want anyone else to have you" kind of love. The kind of love that makes me want to do the exact opposite of whatever he asks. So after the club closed, I took her home, invited her into my bed. She was ravenous. It wasn't just sex or tequila, she consumed my thoughts, my marijuana stash, my peace of mind. She raided my closet, stole my favorite thigh-high boots. When she forged my name on checks, I forgave her. When she rearranged my furniture, re-hung all the art, I looked the other way. And when Pete snuck into the bedroom one midnight, begged for forgiveness, wanted a threesome, I welcomed him. Look, I know it's crazy, but none of this mattered. What mattered was how she sang love songs in the shower. What mattered was that first night, at the Candlelight Lounge, how she stood in the doorway after her set, backlit and dangerous, beautiful.

Alexis Rhone Fancher

CRICKETS

In all these days and years, the only thing
I've learned is a poem needs an engine.
Not a newscaster with ski-slope hair but colorful
sweaters from old dead aunts, penumbra of dust motes,
crumpled *Kleenex,* the frayed edges of gossip. A poem
is about all the things that happen in the meantime
while you are airing the pillows, driving a carpool.
All you missed staring right at what the future
knows and won't tell you. There is a radio dial
we can go and listen to all of us breathing together,
rubbing our chasm of souls in an all-night diner.
A poem needs magic, a bell, a hammer, a noise inside
noise. Never the same thing twice. Only the pathos
that comes over a crowd, the sound of night
eavesdropping on the day. Listen to the glyphs
branches make on a moonlit night. A poem tenders
no apologies for bad haircuts. It will howl
with all your stray dogs in the alleyways of cigarette butts.
A poem needs an engine, not to be sedate as *arts and crafts,*
glue made with water and flour. No, it needs the wheels
to spin in dirt, where someone is kissing
for the first time. It needs a wine glass stomped on
at a wedding, even if it ends in divorce.

Cynthia Atkins

DOUBLE-TIMED AT THE NICKEL DINER

Clare raised the Coke to her lips. Took a swig. Mouthed the words: *Wanna get outta here, baby?* I watched as she rammed her tongue into the bottle for emphasis, her blue eyes fixed on my brown ones. No mistaking that, I thought. I'd waited all my life for a girl like Clare, wild as the wind. The girl my mama warned me about. My best friend Terry's girl. Terry was sitting right next to her, for crissake! And she, acted like he wasn't. Clare had a habit of sucking her left thumb. An oral fixation, always something in her mouth. In my dreams, my cock was in her mouth; I'd wake up sticky and spent. Now she was making noises like she wanted me for real, and I admit, I felt qualmish. I was raised better. And Terry? He was like a brother. But that girl had me by the balls, mesmerized. Her long, dark hair, framed her face, flowed past her tits, fragrant, like night blooming jasmine. *Hey, Terry,* I said, to break Clare's spell. *Wadda ya wanna do now?* Terry shrugged, intent on finishing his burger. Idiot. Never could see what was right in front of him. I watched him chew. Clare watched the clock on the diner's wall. *Tick tock. Tick tock,* she said.

Alexis Rhone Fancher

CONTRONYM DINER

Because I pulled back my name
from his tongue to ask what broke me
          in two—what turns a heart from
star dust to chemical warfare?
Because *left* means both *remained*
and *departed*. Our bodies inflict dents
in the sofa, then disappear.
I know that lost doll in the road
          broken beyond repair.
He found me in hell. I was a road-side bomb
in a war zone. At 15, my parents junked
my belongings on the molten mown lawn.
          I've learned recovery depends
on the thrifty pockets of grief. Before me,
all the women catching a floor-length gown on fire,
          burning houses down. In the meantime
of our lives, so many grave
mistakes are made. Because *bound* means
heading to a destination and being *restrained*.
The man across the table
from me has simple plans.
          He wants it clean. He feeds me soup.
He takes me home, pays the rent. He muzzles
this voice, tamps me down like pipe tobacco.
Gasoline pours on the blueprints of all my plans.
Earth is a portal, I dig and dig—
my ruby lipstick stamps DNA on all
the coffee mugs. *Bolt* means to *secure* or *flee*.

Cynthia Atkins

IN THE DRINK

They've blockaded the beach. The parking lot, chained. *Forbidden.* Like at your house. Changed locks. Restraining order. *Misunderstanding,* I tell the judge. Why does no one believe me? I sneak onto the empty pier where we'd stroll. Lie down, head vised between two concrete posts. The murky water, just a splash below, seems impenetrable as your indifference. I can make out seaweed silhouetted against the dark, undulating current. Mackerel pulse silver. Waves soft-slap against the pier, a lull so docile you'd never imagine their rage. Kicked up by a storm, tossed by an aberrant Sea-Doo. Like you, last night, a tempest I reduced to a squall. Cradled till you realized it was me. Is this what you want? To fuck you and then disappear? I ease my body between the posts, shimmy until I feel the spray, my hair a tangle in the wind. I overheard you on the phone: *If I could put a return label on her marked "broken" and ship her ass back, I would.* Someone's killing peacocks, their bodies bob the harbor, feathers broken, snapped.

Alexis Rhone Fancher

MY PRIVACY SETTINGS

Once my numbers landed
on the balcony of the *Lorraine Hotel*—
famous for only one thing—Martin Luther King
left his last vowels on a portal of air.
      My settings sat next to his motel key
on the bureau, a memory of a memory.
My naked numbers hold a toxic
code to many voluminous sorrows.
Me, myself and I—
O holy dancer, defiled by a loser with
no dress code. His foot made of cheap leather.
      He took the tooth right from
my smile. How an oppressor flings shame
like a trophy. All the balloons
I let go of were full of helium and hope.
      I held vigil over my secret girl crush on Angelica,
my best friend. She said she couldn't
come to my 8th birthday party on that April day,
as tulips came up with like anklets.
      The mystery of her dark skin glow.
A man that she didn't know was shot
on a balcony, and so she couldn't come?—
A preacher man, a friend, a song-bird to my family.
      All assassins are bad boys
going rogue, a shoot-out might kill off their own
inner monsters?—I wished on candles.
At musical chairs, all the kids went round & round
& round with my dizzy settings—out of breath,
misery and sadness offer up their seats.

Cynthia Atkins

THIS POEM IS MADE UP

for the man
whose mother wanted a girl.
This poem is rage. Cage.
Dress up.
This poem is bad intentions.
This poem cannot be made right.
Like some makeover.
Or the man in the dress.
This poem is for the woman
who loved him still.
This poem refuses to lie.
This is how he makes her up.
Because mother.
Because dead ringer.
Is this how you like it?
he asks them both
but not at the same time.
This poem is down low,
is the man's made up life.
How he's barely in it.
This poem refuses to loft.
This poem is for the man
and his mother.
How they pass it down.
Mother to son.
Husband to victim.
How they escape.
But don't.
Because you can't
make these things up.

Alexis Rhone Fancher

MOTHS

I want to write a poem that has not one seed
of grief, is not a pocket or vestibule for tragedy. I want

my cavities to growl and ooze with a hypnotic sweetness—
in the flickering din of a summer night,

diaphanous and full of trill, like the crystal-clear idea that comes
after waking from the duende of sleep. Now the coffee is stirred,

a reflective ping from the deep mouths of spoons. The inner flutter
dispatched by a DJ with an all-nite radio show, slingin' lofty tunes,

making my crinkled skin downy, old as a shirt washed
too many times. Insect wings fling into pig-tails, girlish in the wind.

A world where no one has a curfew or a coffin. I want to write the skiff
of that poem, but I hear a racket on the other side of town, in kitchens,

where mothers and moths congregate under lit fixtures of civilization.
Meanwhile, dark bats in basements, their sons are cleaning their guns.

Cynthia Atkins

FIRE & ICE

Oh, Annie! I hang your portrait in every place I call home. Your eyes follow me, pin me down, like you know something I don't. I can't forget how you show up at my door, dirty-blonde hair in two long braids, heavy make-up on your pale face. *Revlon's Fire & Ice,* you say when I complement your lips. *My mother wore that color,* I want to say but don't, afraid to kill the mood. You're dressed in an old-fashioned white lace gown that covers neck to ankle. Chaste, until you step into the light and the gown turns miraculously transparent. You're naked underneath, the outline of your body, those tennis-toned arms, the way your dark nipples poke through lace. You are usually so shy, half hidden behind your husband, Jonathan, all six foot four of him. When I look for him in the doorway, you smile. *It's just you and me,* you say, like you planned it. *Jonathan's in the kitchen with Eric.* I pull you into the studio, lower the grey seamless backdrop, ready the lights, touch up your already torrid lips, wipe an errant stroke of liner off your lower lid. I want to kiss you, but instead, I hide behind the camera, desperate to finger your left nipple jutting through the lace, a bullseye. You smell like *Evening In Paris.* I long to take you to bed, strip the gown from your body, revel in your nakedness. But I keep thinking of your shady husband and my shady husband, how they might come in at any moment and get the wrong idea. How they're out in the kitchen, guzzling beer, thick as thieves, always plotting their next score. How they'll make a big haul dealing coke to the Angels or maybe selling guns or diamonds, move us all to Costa Rica and go straight till the money runs out.

Alexis Rhone Fancher

SELF-PORTRAIT WITH ELEGY

This is what I would like to remember. The entire room
fuselage and the sky a circumference of hair ribbons
and constellations—our manes wide as the curtains.
Fingers connected the dots and stars with a horse
on my back, follicles lift the brunt

of our history. I painted out the voices, the DNA
of x and y's. Inside the womb, the *Ouija* board of portents,
I hid in the shadows of the unborn. Colors, feral arguments
in the barn of our bedroom where sibling love painted a canvas.

My sister used to tickle my back at night, bring me pretzels thick
with salt. Sister love—part hearts, part arsenic. Like a wicked
nurse checking for a fever, her pinky scraped my flesh. My
freckles dabbed, as if a painter were applying the last strokes.

We were told God would be looking in on us—the fish tank
hummed as fish-eyes bulged into two drunk uncles
leering at our see-thru nightgowns, with flammable gills.
We kept a diary, a pact, a closer look inside our
flowered zippered suitcases, with a lock and key.

She was the painter. I am the survivor—
our eyelashes almost touched.

Cynthia Atkins

ACKNOWLEDGMENTS

Grateful acknowledgment is made to the editors of the following journals in which these works, or earlier versions of them, first appeared:

Cynthia Atkins:
Pine Hills Review: "Contronym Diner"
Rust + Moth: "Moths"
Psaltery & Lyre: "Self-Portrait With Elegy"
SWWIM: "Jewish Singles"
Indianapolis Review: "Diminution, 11 AM"
Night Heron Barks: "Crickets"
Vox Populi: "Social Distancing"
The American Journal of Poetry: "Nine Un-Lives"
The Lily Poetry Review: "My Privacy Settings"
Anti-Heroin Chic: "When the Wells Run Dry"

Alexis Rhone Fancher:
NYQ Magazin:e "We Are All Hopper Paintings Now"
Meat For Tea: "Self-Quarantine Day 240"
Honorable Mention *Steve Kowit Poetry Prize:* "Identity Theft"
The American Journal of Poetry: "Bad Mother"
RATTLE, Poets Respond: "Roadkill, San Pedro"
Book of Matches: "Friday Night at the Candlelight Lounge"
MacQueen's Quinterly: "Double-Timed at the Nickel Diner"
Slipstream: "In the Drink"
Making Up Picture Show Press: "This Poem is Made Up"
Panoply Magazine: "Fire & Ice"

Alexis Rhone Fancher is published in *Best American Poetry*, *Rattle*, *Hobart*, *Verse Daily*, *Plume*, *Tinderbox*, *Cleaver*, *Diode*, *The American Journal of Poetry*, *Spillway*, *Nashville Review*, *Poetry East*, *Gargoyle*, *Duende*, and elsewhere. She's authored six poetry collections, most recently *Junkie Wife* (Moon Tide Press, 2018) and *The Dead Kid Poems* (KYSO Flash Press, 2019). *EROTIC: New & Selected* (NYQ Books) dropped in March 2021. Coming in 2022 and 2023, *Stiletto Killer* (in Italian) from Edizioni Ensemble, Italia, and *BRAZEN*, Alexis's next full-length erotic collection, again by NYQ Books. A coffee table book of Alexis' portraits of Southern California poets will be published in 2023 by Moon Tide Press. Alexis's photographs are featured worldwide, including the covers of *Witness*, *Spillway*, and *The Pedestal Magazine*. A multiple Pushcart Prize and Best of the Net nominee, Alexis is poetry editor of *Cultural Daily*. She and her husband, Fancher, live and frolic on the bluffs of San Pedro, California, overlooking the Pacific Ocean. They have an incredible view. www.alexisrhonefancher.com

Cynthia Atkins is the author of *Psyche's Weathers*, *In The Event of Full Disclosure* (CW Books, 2007), and *Still-Life With God* (Saint Julian Press, 2020). Her work has appeared in numerous journals, including *Alaska Quarterly Review*, *BOMB*, *Cleaver Magazine*, *Diode*, *Florida Review*, *Green Mountains Review*, *Rust + Moth*, *North American Review*, *Seneca Review*, *Thrush*, *Tinderbox*, and *Verse Daily*. She was formerly the assistant director for the Poetry Society of America and has taught English and Creative Writing, most recently at Blue Ridge Community College. She is an Interviews Editor for *American Microreviews and Interviews*. Atkins earned her MFA from Columbia University and fellowships and prizes from Bread Loaf Writers' Conference, Virginia Center for the Creative Arts, The Writer's Voice, and Writers@Work. Atkins lives on the Maury River of Rockbridge County, Virginia, with artist Phillip Welch and their family. More work and info at: www.cynthiaatkins.com.

Made in the USA
Middletown, DE
28 August 2022

72549508R00027